NAMES ON THE LAND

Stories behind the Street Names
of San Fernando Valley

ROBERT LIVINGSTON

ISBN
978-1-964035-97-0 (Paperback)
978-1-964035-98-7 (eBook)

To The Old Guys

Table of Contents

OTHER BOOKS BY THE AUTHOR viii
INTRODUCTION –NAMES ON THE LAND i
PROLOGUE – THE BARREN MAP iii
CHAPTER I – ADRIFT 1
CHAPTER 2 – GETTING STARTED 9
CHAPTER 3 – THE OLD GUYS 16
CHAPTER 4 – THE REST OF THE GUYS 28
CHAPTER 5 – NAMING STREETS 35
CHAPTER 6 – OTHER STREET NAMES 44
CHAPTER 7 – THE MAP 58
CHAPTER 8 – WIDER SPACES 60
CHAPTER 9– RESEDA AND MORE 68
CHAPTER 10 – CHATSWORTH 76
CHAPTER 11 – SYLMAR 83
CHAPTER 12 – PACOIMA 88
CHAPTER 13 – SAN FERNANDO 92
CHAPTER 14 – MISSION HILLS 100
CHAPTER 15 – NORTH HILLS 105
CHAPTER 16 – PANORAMA CITY 110
CHAPTER 17– WINNETKA 117
CHAPTER 18 – WOODLAND HILLS 120
CHAPTER 19 – SNOW IN THE VALLEY 125
CHAPTER 20 – CANOGA PARK 129
CHAPTER 21 – VAN NUYS 142
CHAPTER 22 – IN THE LIMELIGHT 147
CHAPTER 23 – SUNLAND-TUJUNGA 159
CHAPTER 24 – BURBANK 168
CHAPTER 25 – GLENDALE 178
CHAPTER 26 – TOLUCA LAKE 191
CHAPTER 27 – STUDIO CITY 198

CHAPTER 28 – SHERMAN OAKS 206
CHAPTER 29 – LAKE VIEW TERRACE 213
CHAPTER 30 – MOVIE MAGIC AND THE VALLEY 219
CHAPTER 31 – COOL MUSEUMS IN THE VALLEY 234
CHAPTER 32 – MUSEUMS IN MISSION HILLS 247
CHAPTER 33 – LEGACY 252

POSTSCRIPT **253**

OTHER BOOKS BY THE AUTHOR

LEAPING INTO THE SKY
FLEET
AXIS ALLY
A TARNISHED ROSE
AMERICAN STORIES
BLUE JACKETS
THE SAILOR AND TEACHER
HARLEM ON THE WESTERN FRONT
THE FORGOTTEN CHAPLAIN
IN THE WAKE OF THE EMPRESS OF CHINA
THE CONSPIRACY OF 1910 TO SAVE THE WORLD
TRAVELS WITH ERNIE
A DEAN'S LIFE

INTRODUCTION –NAMES
ON THE LAND

This is a story of a few street names in the San Fernando Valley, the suburban landscape north of Los Angeles. Where possible, three questions prompted this work. First, why was a street so named? Second, who named the street? Third, how was the area's history and culture tied to the street sign?

Motorists and pedestrians seldom ask these questions. As fellow travelers, however, they may access a dashboard navigation system or an Apple cellphone to reach a location. Much like wallpaper in a room, little attention is paid to street signs. They exist in a time-warp of anonymity, seen but not comprehended, metallic letters fluttering in the wind or tightly riveted to a rusting iron pole. They are everywhere, well over 178,000 street signs in Los Angeles, by way of example, to mark the city's 40,000 intersections. Approximately 50,000 street signs are in the San Fernando Valley. They are everywhere, used by everyone from the Postal Service to Amazon delivery trucks to seniors looking for the latest Fish and Hook outlet. Magazines and newspapers find their way to an address, just as those attending a birthday party do. A "blind date" typically involves meeting at a specific location.

The street signs are everywhere. They quietly, if not stoically, assist us through our day with their names and numbers.

Street signs are similar to postage stamps. In miniature form, they acknowledge and celebrate the past, reminding us of those who forged our history.

This story, though tempted to identify each street sign in the San Fernando Valley, must necessarily focus on a more manageable effort. The selected street signs in Northridge were first researched, and their histories were revealed. Other areas of the Valley (as the natives call it) were also investigated, including Sherman Oaks, Sunland–Tujunga, Canoga Park, Granada Hills, and Woodland Hills. Given its proximity to Hollywood and the magic of movies, that connection to the Valley was also explored.

Always, the focus was on the human drama behind the sign that led to its naming. Hopefully, that goal has been accomplished.

PROLOGUE – THE BARREN MAP

The land was there. It had form and presence. It was a time when the North American continent was largely unexplored and nameless. The great mountains were present and without names. The rivers flowed unceasingly in every direction yet were nameless. Great stretches of the prairie land existed, as did innumerable valleys and lakes, all without a name. At some point in the distant past, humanity entered the picture, those we refer to as "Indigenous People" or "Native Americans." Their presence began the process of naming the land. Initially, they may have lacked a written language, so names had to be remembered by associating them with something of significance. Perhaps a small lake or a fast-running stream where the fish abounded… Possibly a jagged peak that resonated spiritually with the tribe… Perhaps where the buffalo pounded the turf or where the beaver built their earthworks… All these were places to be recalled and thus demanded a name for future reference.

Those who came before us gave names to rivers, mountains, towns, and, in time, to streets in cities. The land was no longer barren of human notations. The mountains were named, the Appalachians in the east and the Rockies in the west. The Great Lakes, which were explored and navigated, include Lake Superior, Lake Michigan, Lake Huron, Lake Ontario, and Lake Erie. Out west, Lake Tahoe was named, as was Lake Okeechobee in Florida, and Travis Lake in Texas. The Great Plains stretched from horizon to horizon and were named as such.

The naming process encompasses wider areas of human habitat, as with the names of our states or counties, or the 50 stars on the flag fluttering in the wind. The names became commonplace. They appeared on the map, their longitude and latitude precisely noted by cartographers. The names evolved out of the interaction of culture, history, and the unceasing human drama played out by those who explored the land and felt the impulse to fill in the blank map.

In 1682, the La Salle expedition explored the lower Mississippi River, from the mouth of the Illinois River to the Gulf of Mexico. On April 9, 1682, René-Robert Cavelier, Sieur de La Salle, prayed to God and claimed the Mississippi Basin for France. In doing so, he gave La Louisiane to the land in honor of Louis XIV. Between 1775 and 1776, Juan Bautista de Anza led a colonizing expedition through the Southwest and to what would later be known as Alta California. He carried the banner of New Spain and a lexicon of Spanish names bestowed upon the land. Between 1804 and 1806, a military expedition led by Captain Meriwether Lew and Lieutenant William Clark explored the Louisiana Purchase at the behest of President Thomas Jefferson. From East Saint Louis to Astoria, Oregon, they filled in the first rudimentary maps of the West with names. In Washington State, it was Camp Disappointment on the edge of the continent fronting the Pacific Ocean. In Montana, it was Pompey's Pillar, a rock formation of sandstone that defied gravity and reached the heavens.

A legacy of names constantly reminded us of those who contributed to the naming process and all the locales that describe our varied landscape of places and people. That being the case, for example, we have contemporary locations such as the Golden Triangle, the Loop, the Back Bay, and the Gas House District that remind us of the naming process. In San Francisco, two edifices dominate the skyline: the Bridge and the Golden Gate, names etched in our collective memory. And in Southern California near Los Angeles, there is The Valley.

The Loop refers to the heart of downtown Chicago, bounded by the Chicago River to the north and west, Harrison Street to the south, and Lake Michigan to the east. It is a densely populated area of 1.56 square miles that contains the famous Chicago River Walk. It is called the Loop because of the elevated train tracks that form a loop around the city's central business section. Each day, thousands are transported in Carl Sandburg's *Chicago*.

Hog Butcher for the World,
Tool maker, Stacker of Wheat,
Player with Railroads and the Nation's
Freight Handler
Stormy, husky, brawling,
City of Big Shoulders…

The Golden Triangle is a region in Mississippi formed by the cities of Columbus, Starkville, and West Point. The name evolved from a need to attract businesses, spur economic development, and foster cooperation among local communities. That has been the outcome. High-tech industries have migrated to the area, providing good jobs and revenues for municipalities. Texas also has a "triangle." It is defined by the cities of Beaumont, Port Arthur, and Orange, all of which are related to oil strikes. Montana comes into the picture with a region known for wheat farming, tied to the towns of Shelby, Great Falls, and Havre. Each "triangle" is noted for its cooperative planning in developing an economic plan, responsive to local history yet looking ahead for the next generation of its citizens.

The Back Bay is an area tied to Boston, Massachusetts. The boundaries are tied to the Charles River to the north, the Massachusetts Turnpike to the south, and the Public Garden to the east. To the west, Charles Gate East completes the border. Back Bay refers to a small inlet or bay in a geographical area. It is also a specific neighborhood. The area was originally a tidal body of water. An extensive landfill began in the 1850s. Over 450 acres of usable land were created, and new names appeared on city streets.

The Gas House District is a historic neighborhood in Manhattan. It is located on the east side near the 19th and 20th streets. In 1842, the first gas storage tank was erected at East 23rd Street. Over time, other gas tanks were constructed, giving rise to the name "Gashouse District." Due to its industrial history, the area has been relatively impoverished, attracting immigrant populations, including the Irish, Italians, and Germans. The location was notorious for its crimes, including the infamous "Gas House Gang."

The Bridge is commonly referred to as the San Francisco-Oakland Bay Bridge. To those who live in the city, it is simply "The Bridge." It was actually constructed in two segments: a suspension bridge between Oakland and Yerba Buena Island and a suspension span from the island to San Francisco. Including approaches and the toll plaza, the structure is 8.4 miles in length. It opened in 1936 for $77 million.

The Golden Gate is an awe-inspiring sight, an engineering marvel, a bridge spanning 1.70 miles between San Francisco and Marin County, and all roads to Northern California. The suspension bridge, painted in its iconic orange color, is named after the Golden Gate Strait, the narrow passage connecting San Francisco Bay to the Pacific Ocean. The water under the structure reaches a depth of about 371 feet. For the city named after Saint Francis, the bridge is affectionately known as the Golden Gate; that is, a visual poem in steel, bolted together by hot rivets.

The Valley refers to the San Fernando Valley, a subdivision paradise for developers just north of Los Angeles proper. Once the pastoral land of ranches, farms, and groves of citrus fruits, as well as stretches of wheat and barley, the Valley is now a vast, sprawling example of suburbia, with single-family homes marking the landscape and freeways connecting a multitude of postal zones to Los Angeles. It is the middle-class dream: a three-bedroom house, a BBQ in the backyard, a garage with a new Ford or Chevy, and a front lawn lush, green, and inviting.

This was, of course, the history of the West, and more specifically, that land later known as California, with a vast valley to be named the San Fernando Valley. Into the history of these geographical units came the Spanish, and later those from Mexico. And with them came the need to name all that they saw. Out of this would come empires and nations, states, counties, towns, and cities, each requiring a name to denote its existence and its place on a map.

Perhaps it all began with this process of naming, at least for the Spanish on the eastern coast of the continent, long before there was an

America. The date was April 2, 1513, and the European navigators and explorers were about to end the namelessness of what was before them.

Days earlier, Juan Ponce de Leon had sailed from Puerto Rico with three ships seeking honor and wealth in equal proportions. He came to a coastline, suggesting something more than an island, or a sandbank, not even a key. The land stretched out into a low plain and groves of trees, and fauna of all sorts, all green with the April sun. What he saw was a land of flowers, lush in color. There was no priest with him to tell him which saint should be remembered on the second day of the new month. That being the case, he knew, as a Spanish leader should know, that it was the season of Our Lord's Resurrection, which occurred only six days after the Easter of Flowers. With this in mind, he combined the two occasions. Ponce de Leon named the land Florida to celebrate the "Feast of Flowers."

Naming would be repeated as the Spanish explored the continent. On May 13, 1691, those who named the land reached a small river. It was a day celebrated in honor of Saint Anthony of Padua, the renowned Franciscan friar who assisted the pious. The stream was called San Antonio. Later, a mission would be built, also bearing that name, and in time, a great city would arise, San Antonio.

But where was San Antonio? Over time, the Spanish adopted the word "Texas" from the Indian word "tejas," meaning "friends" or "allies." When the Spanish first heard the phrase "Techas," they thought it referred to the name of a tribe, or possibly a kingdom. The word was a form of greeting that the different tribes used, and now they used it with the bearded ones in armor, glistening swords. In short, it was a salutation.

Earlier, the Spanish arrived in California. In 1595, Sebastian Rodriguez Cermeno made landfall on the California coast before entering an excellent harbor. On November 7, 1595, he took possession of all that he could see. Aboard his ship, which had sailed from Manila, was a Franciscan friar named Francisco. As was the custom, he baptized the land, perhaps pouring water upon it. The bay was named in his honor, San Francisco. The process of naming had come to the "land of dreams." Years later, the city of San Francisco would be named after Saint Francis of Assisi, the patron saint of the Franciscan order. That was in the year 1847. In doing so, the area's first name, Yerba Buena, was scrapped.

In 1781, forty-four settlers, known as "Los Pobladores," founded a settlement named "El Pueblo de Nuestra Señora la Reina de los Ángeles de Porciuncula." Governor Felipe de Neve gave the name. The name translates to "The Town of Our Lady the Queen of the Angels of Porciuncula. As to Porciuncula, the word translates to "little portion" in English, and it refers to a chapel in Assisi, Italy, where Saint Francis began his order. Today, we know the area of Los Angeles, also referred to by its abbreviated name, LA.

If anyone left their mark in naming locations during early Spanish days in California, it was Father Junípero Serra, a missionary of the Franciscan Order. Through his unceasing efforts, he oversaw the planning, construction, and staffing of missions in California. They included: San Diego de Alcala (1769), San Carlos Borromeo (Carmel) in 1770, San Gabriel Arcangel (1771), San Luis Obispo de Tolosa (1772), San Francisco de Asis (1776), San Juan Capistrano (1776), Santa Clara de Asis (1777), and San Buenaventura (1782).

The process of naming is not straightforward. At least initially, no government entity structured the process, although the Spanish were moving in that direction by establishing missions. Sometimes, a quirk of fate intervenes, setting in motion a kaleidoscope of new names, many thought out, while others are the creatures of happenstance. That was the case in California when a glint of ore caught one man's attention.

On January 24, 1848, James W. Marshall discovered gold in the American River at Sutter's Mill in Coloma, California. In doing so, he set off the California Gold Rush and altered the history of the Mexican province, as well as the legacy of its Spanish and Mexican past. Thousands seeking riches crossed the continent by train, stagecoach, mule, and horse. Others sailed from the East Coast around Cape Horn and past the headland of Tierra del Fuego, an archipelago off the southern coast of Chile. Whether by land or sea, the trek to California was difficult, if not treacherous. Once in the gold fields, the miners gave new names to the land.

Poker Flat was located in California's Sierra County. At one time, the small mining community was considered wealthy based on the amount of gold dug from the land or found in the streams. According to local lore, gold was used as poker chips, and that's how the town got its name. During the boom times, the city saw an influx of gamblers and attractive ladies of the night. Reportedly, there were fifteen saloons and casinos where miners could gamble away their hard-earned but temporary wealth. In his short story "The Outcasts of Poker Flat" (1869), Bret Harte gave literary fame to the town.

Angels Camp played a significant role in the "gold rush." The town was founded in 1848 in the middle of the Mother Lode country and was named after Henry Pinkey Angle, who established a trading post there. As in the case of other camps, saloons, gambling, and "tainted ladies" found their way into Angels Camp, which was in Calaveras County. It was situated at the confluence of Angels Creek, China Gulch, and China Creek, and about ten miles from the town of San Andreas. Indeed, gold miners and others brought new names to California, as Mark Twain did in his celebrated short story *The Jumping Frog of Calaveras County* (1865). The story of Jim Smiley and His Jumping Frog still tickles us to this day with its humor and satire.

Placerville, California, was another famous Gold Rush town. Finding gold on the American River cemented its place in history. The town's nickname was "Hangtown." Still another name colored the town's history, "Dry Diggins." A sister locale was El Dorado in the 1850s. It was first named Mud Springs and was known as a watering hole for livestock along the road connecting Sacramento to Placerville.

The "forty-niners" expressed the eternal hope of many to get rich. In the process of doing so, they added to the lexicon of names denoting California's history. They also set in motion the strands of history that would eventually lead to the California Bear Flag Rebellion and later statehood. Where once Spain ruled and later Mexico City, the Yankee now appeared on the scene.

All had contributed to and would continue to contribute to the names on the map. It is an ongoing process that continues to this day, whether to mark a spot on the lunar landscape or to identify a new valley once hidden in the lush foliage of a Central American country. What is discovered requires a name. What is newly built demands a designation. What is envisioned cries out for a moniker. It is the way humanity provided continuity and understanding to its history and what it hopes to achieve in the future. Long ago, Walt Whitman alluded to these themes.

> *I will plant companionship thick as trees along the rivers of*
> *America, and along he shores of the great lakes, and all over The prairies.*
> *I will make inseparable cities, with their arms about each other's necks;*
> *By the love of comrades,*
> *By the manly love of comrades...*
>
> *For you these, from me, O Democracy, to serve you,*
> *For you! For you, I am thrilling these songs,*
> *In the love of comrades,*
> *In the high-towering love of comrades.*

CHAPTER I – ADRIFT

It was a bright, shining day in the San Fernando Valley. A slight breeze rustled through the former California landscape of grapefruit, lemon, and orange groves, all of which were straddled by wheat farmers, herds of cattle, and horse ranches, many of which dated back to Spanish times.

It was a lovely day to be out for a walk, even for a senior in his mid-80s moving carefully down the sidewalk, cane and all, as he tried to avoid a mishap where the concrete resembled ice heaps in Alaska. The Old Guy should have been in good cheer. He had finished off a nice breakfast, consisting of scrambled eggs, potatoes, and two cups of very dark, black coffee —both instant and decaf, of course. Yes, he should have been a happy camper. His wife loved him, his faults and all. The kids and grandchildren were gracious in their affection. His pension program was solvent, and a few CDs were on deposit. Again, he should have been a happy camper.

He wasn't.

He was on his way to see his buddies at Ray's house, just a short jog (if he were so inclined) or stroll (which now preoccupied his new slip-on shoes, a birthday present from his daughter). By all accounts, he should have been in a reasonable frame of mind. The frame was there, but it only enclosed low-keyed anger and mounting frustration.

The Old Guy was depressed and had been for several weeks. Financial problems? That wasn't the case. Troubles with his spouse of 50-plus years or with the kids, now adults and off in the world doing their own thing? Not really. Encountering difficulty accepting the physical challenges of aging? To some extent, yes, but that was not the cause of his grumpy mood. Like most people, he wanted to live forever without growing older, a notion that defied every generation. Of course, he was also aware of an oft-stated

1

cry of senior citizens: "Growing older isn't for sissies." That business he understood, but it really didn't trouble him.

He was afflicted with something more serious than the clock ticking.

The Old Guy was enduring "writer's block!" For many weeks, his creative juices, such as they were, had dried up, leaving him more parched than the sands of Death Valley. He seemed to be experiencing what some called a "persistent inability to write." It wasn't from a lack of motivation, though at times that seemed to be the case. Perhaps, more to the point, it was a dearth of inspiration. Nothing seemed to appeal to him, regardless of the many potential topics he slung at his "little brain cells." No matter how much time he spent before his ancient Apple Mac peering at a blank screen and a blinking cursor, his fingers remained immobilized, glued to the plastic keys, stranded in something akin to being adrift in a mental Sargasso Sea.

How bad was his writer's block? Imagine yourself staring at the curving western wall of Hoover Dam, a concrete barrier holding back the Colorado River. Or perhaps you are at the Panama Canal, peering at the giant locks that lift immense container ships from sea level to the heights of Panama, lock by lock, across the isthmus to link two seas. Concrete everywhere…

In his state, he had more concrete than Home Depot and the DIY stores. That's what he saw on the computer screen: blocks of self-doubt and an increasing inability to write, all very disheartening.

He needed a jolt to pull himself out of these doldrums. He required an epiphany, if you will—something to knock him for a loop. Perhaps an out-of-body experience not brought about by peyote or creativity found in a bottle of Old Turkey. That's what the Old Guy needed, something that would knock the smithereens out of the blocks of concrete still mocking his creative juices.

And that's what happened.

It isn't easy even now to comprehend precisely what occurred. Perhaps the mad gods that influence our fate took pity on the Old Guy. That was one possibility. Maybe it was just serendipity. Out of obscure randomness, the Old Guy stopped while walking at just the right moment and just the right place to rest for a moment. As he sat on a cement wall that kept folks from trampling on a neighbor's garden, he peered at a ubiquitous equivalent of R2-D2, a discolored and somewhat stained city hydrant, tarnished from the sun and rusting in places. Looking at the hydrant, he mused about these little figures found on every street, present and inert, until the clang of fire engines awakened them. He was less than inspired by the little guy with funny knobs that now seemed to be mocking him, at least in an anthropomorphic way. "Hey," it seemed to be saying, "you're close, look around and up. Got it?"

He did.

They looked up at an old street sign, resting on an equally ancient metal pole. It certainly wasn't a rational decision on his part. He was, after all, taking a cue from a hydrant. Nevertheless, he did gaze at the street sign on that fateful day.

He had been on his way to his good friend Ray's house for a meeting with some buddies. It was Tuesday, and time to be with his Old Guy group. Anyway, as he focused on the street sign, an unexpected surge of feelings and thoughts entered his consciousness in what some Buddhists might call a moment of "enlightenment." Starting a little less eloquently but true, his writer's block began to crumble. As he did, he was reminded of the immortal words from the Batman cartoons: SMASH, BANG, POW!

Goodbye Hoover Dam! Adios, the Panama Locks!

HOOVER DAM

PANAMA CANAL

Ray's house in Northridge was just a short walk from where the Old Guy lived, first down Germain Street and then to Canby Street before reaching the corner of Canby and San Jose, and his destination. Just a simple walk, one he had done many times, and literally one you couldn't get lost doing. Head west, turn south, and stop at the corner. Nothing could be easier. True, he had once gotten lost doing this trek. Perhaps he had too many meds that day. Who knows? It wasn't something he discussed in polite company.

This particular day would prove different. Not that he would get lost... Not again... Just the opposite in fact... For reasons he couldn't fully explain, even now so many months later, he stared at the street sign. It was as if the signs were saying, "Hey, you... Yes you... Pause to look at me." First, a fire hydrant had claimed his attention, and now street signs were conversing with him. Had he been in therapy, he would have kept these conversations to himself.

Later, he would look at another sign for San Jose Street. The signs were mesmerizing. They held his attention. Just somewhat weather-beaten signs locked to metal poles, acknowledging a location or to help someone reach a destination, even in the era of Apple navigation systems. He stood transfixed. It wasn't quite a trance. It was more like a meeting of the minds, assuming that inanimate signposts were capable of such a rendezvous. As he gazed, an old memory rose to the surface of his mind, grasping for his consciousness, as if to create a connection between the past and the present.

The Old Guy could almost hear a voice whispering loudly in his mind, "Bob Livingston, pay attention. Remember…"

He took heed.

Years ago, he had read a book titled *Names on the Land*. The author was George R. Stewart, a Professor of English at U.C. Berkley. He had written several books, all of which the Old Guy had read, including three favorites: *Fire, Storm*, and *Names on the Land*.

It was the third book that now claimed his attention. Written during World War II, it was Stewart's effort to remind Americans of their unique history and the country's varied heritages by explaining how our nation's names came about. The book spoke of history, geography, and culture… Quietly, it inspired and nurtured a sense of patriotism for a society at war.

The book had made quite an impression on the Old Guy. It was an exciting narrative of the romance, tragedy, idealism, and humor that describe the process of placing names on the North American landscape over four centuries. It all began with indigenous peoples, whose names were, as Stewart wrote, "often lost, ignored, or vulgarized by the English and the Spanish."

THE AUTHOR

THE BOOK

It was a joy to read, especially if you were a history major in college and later a high school instructor, which the Old Guy had been. Now, as he stood before the street signs, the proverbial light went on. Could he emulate Stewart's work? Not, of course, on a national scope, but perhaps something closer to home. Might he write about his own neighborhood and the street signs situated on every corner? Could he expand his literary effort to the San Fernando Valley?

Could he explain how the names on the signs came to be and what they meant? With so many street signs in Los Angeles, and many thousands of them in the San Fernando Valley, where would he begin? The answer was, of course, right in front of him. His research would start with the three street signs leading to Ray's adobe (more colorful than the word house). And then, if things worked out, he would learn and write about the streets where his close buddies lived. After that…

The concrete blocks that had cluttered the Old Guy's were gone. Motivation and inspiration took over, necessitating a substantial amount of research. He felt good to be before the old Mac with the cursor no longer saying, "Look, the way this works, you dance on the keys, and the screen glows with sentences that make sense. Got it?"

The Old Guy did. In doing so, he recalled another quote from Stewart.

"We all want to see the unseen and know the unknown."

CHAPTER 2 – GETTING STARTED

Research takes time. One has to be patient. Unfortunately, the street signs provided only a name. That's it. No background, no fine print. Nothing about the meaning of the name on the street sign. There is no hint as to who named the street or why. Notta…

The street signs were stoic, seeming immune to the concerns of mortal beings, almost as if to say, "Others have passed by, and more will come, but my secrets I grudgingly protect from your inquiring minds."

That was the challenge then: unlocking the past and bringing to light stories that were unknown to most.

The Old Guy would have to sneak into the CSUN library as a senior to access resource materials. He did. And, of course, he embarrassed himself. He asked a lovely young lady where the Dewey Decimal cards were located. She gave him a perplexed look, one you might save for a modern Rip Van Winkle who had just awakened from a long sleep. With a sympathetic look, she pointed to her digital watch. That brought a bemused but foolish response from the Old Guy. Taking pity on him, she flourished her late-model Apple phone, saying, "It's a digital world out there. Let's go over to the computers."

That being the case, the Old Guy dove headlong into the digital world, seeking enlightening information on the Internet, beginning with basic facts and later curious stories about personalities long lost to time. It turned out to be quite a dive. Over time, the gathering of this and that began to make sense and provided a path for writing.

The Old Guy began on Germain Street in Northridge, California, a suburb in the northwestern quadrant of the Valley (as locals call the San

Fernando Valley). For this first effort, he didn't want to stray too far from home. A risk taker he was not.

Piecing together lonely facts from here and there, he arrived at this. The San Fernando Valley was once home to Eugene Germain, an adventurous young man born in Avenches, Switzerland, in 1847 (1847-1907). He was, it should be noted, of the Jewish faith. Twenty-two years later, he arrived in Los Angeles. That was in 1847. Over time, he entered the grocery business. He did well, providing provisions to early settlers from the East and selling to one Pio Pico, the last governor of Mexican-controlled California (1801-1894). Germain Pio Pico purchased eggs, mackerel, and crackers. That was, of course, before your local Vons.

In 1882, Germain formed the Germain Fruit Company. The company did well, selling citrus fruit to those east of the Mississippi. In 1871, he founded the Germain Seed Company, which later became the Germain Seed and Plant Company in 1889. The company was headquartered in Van Nuys, California. Germain died in 1909. He left an estate worth over $ 2 million. That's a lot of seed. This being the case, it was understandable that a street would be named after this businessman from the old country. It is unknown who actually called the street after him. The best bet was someone in the City Planning Department.

EUGENE GERMAIN

A GERMAIN SEED TRUCK

DON PIO de JESUS PICO

Canby Street proved to be a real challenge. Two possibilities, however, emerged regarding the street's meaning. Canby was a boy's name of Middle English origin. It can also refer to a "settlement near reeds," or a "farm near the reeds." The second choice is much more colorful, although it is challenging to relate to the semi-arid landscape of the Valley—time to head north, way north. See what you think.

Canby is a town in Modoc County, approximately 17 miles west of Alturas, Oregon. Population: a few more than 200 souls. The first Post Office was opened there in 1874. The town was named in honor of General Edward Canby, a decorated Civil War veteran (1817-1873). Unfortunately, General Canby was shot and killed by a Modoc tribal leader named Captain Jack while the two were trying to end the Modoc

War of the 1870s. The tribal leader's real name was Kientpoos Kintpoos (1837-1873). Perhaps some resident of the Valley (or civil engineer) knew of the General's exploits and undoing. In the absence of more information, those are two plausible explanations for the Canby Street sign.

GENERAL CANBY

MAKING A PEACE TREATY

CAPTAIN JACK

In Spanish, San Jose Street is named after Saint Joseph, who is considered the patron saint of pioneers and travelers. In Spanish, "San" means "Saint" (the masculine noun) or "Santa" (the feminine noun). San can also refer to that which is holy or sacred. Saint Joseph's name can also be invoked to protect you against sudden death, drowning, poisoning, or falling into the hands of your enemies. Whether or not that also refers to contemporary political parties is an open question. And one more thing... According to the New Testament, Saint Joseph was married to Mary, the mother of Jesus.

The City of San Jose also bears Saint Joseph's name. The city was founded as El Pueblo de San Jose de Guadalupe on November 29, 1777, near the Guadalupe River by Captain Juan Bautista de Anza (1736-1788). Governor Felipe de Neve (1724-1784) had authorized the establishment of California's first civil settlement. That job was left to Lieutenant Jose Joaquin Moraga (1745-1785) to do with 14 settlers. It was the first town in the Spanish colony of Nueva California. Neva can be translated to snow and is associated with purity, beauty, and tranquility.

ANZA, THE EXPLORER, THE SAINT

It is assumed that those who named the street were aware of these connections, our Spanish legacy in California, and the westward expansion of Europeans across the continent. That assumption seems sound.

The Old Guy was on a roll. It was enjoyable learning about these streets and the possible reasons they were given their names. Indeed, the process of researching and writing was quite stimulating and similarly addictive. It was a little like being held hostage in a *Mary Sees* candy store. Every new uncovered fact was tasty, leaving one desiring to try another morsel. In any event, this led to a decision. The Old Guy would expand his immediate horizons.

He would research the street names of his close buddies, the guys he met with each week. However, first, a brief introduction is necessary for those unfamiliar with this motley group of grizzled seniors.

A Personal Note

A strange feeling overcame me as I walked through the neighborhood, glancing furtively at the street signs. I felt like I was entering a shadowy world of hidden secrets and the ghostly lives of those long gone, but not before they left their indelible mark on the land. I tried not to think of myself as an intruder, a transient spectator peering into the cobwebs of history. I wanted... No... I needed to find an intimacy with the past, something beyond mere names and the kaleidoscope of events that forged their lives.

Another thought found its way into my consciousness, one that I had memorized years earlier after reading George Stewart's seminal work, Earth Abides. It seemed to direct me to what lay ahead.

"Men go and come, but earth abides."

CHAPTER 3 – THE OLD GUYS

Each week and every Tuesday morning, the Old Guy met with a group of seniors to discuss whatever came to mind. They call themselves the Old Guys. They meet and talk. Sometimes, political issues clamor for discussion. That was most of the time. In that sense, the guys were a kind of fraternal group enmeshed in current events. At other times, it's just chitchat about our kids and grandchildren or the cost of a homeowner's policy in fire-prone Southern California.

Conspicuously, as a group, the old guys made a real effort to avoid discussing their medical maladies or torrid romances from years past. Outside of these areas, all topics are possible. You get the idea. They freelance. It should be noted that they do so without rancor and always with a desire to learn from each other. And, of course, one other thing should be mentioned. The group is quite capable of resolving the world's problems and has often done so. Unfortunately, the world usually pays little heed to its collective wisdom.

Let's begin with a word about Ray. You know... The guy who lives at Canby and San Jose... This lanky ex-Marine is the guy in our group who keeps us organized. Since we meet in different homes each week, Ray provides addresses and directions via our cell phones and computers to keep us from getting lost and to avoid areas like Barstow, California, and Searchlight, Nevada. I should add that Ray has a fantastic memory, leaving many to say, "Ray, how did you know that?" often.

Ray spent a lifetime in manufacturing, much of it in the aerospace industry. We go to Ray for his views on that. He's also the person we turn to for information on military-related issues.

Next up, Leo. He lives on Garden Grove Avenue, not far from Germain Street and Ray's place. Leo was a UCLA graduate with a sly sense of humor and a fascinating work history. He was in the music business for years before transitioning into the car repair industry. Not a chop shop... Just repairs at a fair price... Recently, he took art lessons, and his efforts have been impressive. Now as to his street sign...

It turns out that Garden Grove refers to an abundance of citrus groves that once existed in the San Fernando Valley, including oranges, lemons, and grapefruit. As for the term' grove,' it is an Old English, Scottish, and Anglo-Saxon surname. The term originated from the Norman French "Le Groux," a name for someone who lived near a grove or thicket, that is, someone living in an area with a group of trees standing together.

Naturally, there is another possibility. In 1874, Dr. Alonzo Gerry Cook (1839-1932) donated land to establish the village that is now known as Garden Grove, California. The substantial donation was intended for the construction of a school and a civic center. Dr. Cook had bought the land, some 160 acres, years earlier from the Abel Stearns Ranch.

Abel Stearns, it turns out, was quite a guy (1796-1871). He arrived in Pueblo de Los Angeles, Alta, California, in 1829 and became a large landowner and cattle rancher over time. In Los Angeles, he received the right to build a warehouse at San Pedro, the nearest seaport to the youthful settlement. In time, he established a stagecoach route that connected San Pedro Bay with the Los Angeles pueblo. In 1842, he bought his first rancho, Rancho Los Alamitos, located between LA and the harbor. It was a sizeable purchase, 28,000 acres for cattle to roam. In 1842, Sterns completed the first shipment of gold to the U.S. Mint valued at $19 per ounce. It was deposited in the Philadelphia Mint. He did all this in addition to his other business endeavors. Not bad for a guy born in Lunenburg, Massachusetts.

Perhaps in naming Leo's street, someone was aware of the good doctor and more...

DR. ALONZO COOK, ABEL STEARNS

––––––––––––––––

To get from Leo's home to the Old Guy's residence by a slightly different route, you have to cross Etiwanda Street. Nice sounding name… As you might expect, the Old Guy wanted to know how that name came about.

Etiwanda was named after the Etiwanda Native American tribe that inhabited the shores of Lake Michigan. This, however, is where things get complicated. The Etiwanda Indian tribe is not recognized as a Native American tribe. When non-indigenous people (white trappers and settlers) entered the area, they appropriated the word Etiwanda from the term "Ittiwan." That said, how did the name get to the Golden State?

In 1881, two brothers, George and William Chaffey, purchased land from Joseph Garcia, a retired sea captain. Apparently, the brothers were from Canada and were aware of the Etiwanda tribe. They planned a town that eventually became Rancho Cucamonga.

As an aside… In doing so, they established the Etiwanda Water Company and designed an irrigation system that became the standard for water system management in southern California. Two other innovations are part of the town's history. The first long-distance telephone call in Southern California was made in 1882, connecting San Bernardino to the Etiwanda Water Company. On December 4, 1882, the Chaffey home was illuminated by the community's first electric lights.

Someone in the City's Planning Department must have been aware of this history.

GEORGE (1848-1932) AND WILLIAM (1855-192 CHAFFEY

————————————

Living near Old Guy's simple abode is another member of the group. That's Rony. He lives on Chatsworth Street between Etiwanda Street and Reseda Boulevard. Rony is the most mysterious guy in the group. That's not meant in a sinister sense. He worked in Los Angeles and throughout the world. As to what he did remains open to question. Lots of speculation…

Rony is also a follower of the Zoroaster faith and its founder, Zarathushtra. He makes yearly trips to India, his country of origin. Exactly how he spends his time in the once prime jewel of the British Empire is unknown. In any event, he is a great guy who expounds endlessly (and wisely) on the challenges America faces with China.

ZARATHUSHTRA

As to Chatsworth Street... What's the story here? The area known as Chatsworth, California, originated in 1888 as Chatsworth Park. That year, the event was recorded in the Los Angeles County Recorder's Office. A fellow by the name of George R. Crow (1864-1909) did it. He was part of a group that paid Benjamin F. Porter $500,000 for the 19,417 acres. Porter was a large landowner (1808-1868). The San Fernando Valley Improvement Company now owned the real estate. One of its directors was William Booth Barber (1819-1901). As it turns out, he was born in Eckington, Derbyshire, England, just a few miles from Chatsworth House. This abode was the ancestral home of the Duke of Devonshire. Barber, it appears, claimed the name for the sprawling northwest area of the Valley. This happened in 1917. One could argue the British, through Barber, were quietly retaking at least one colonial possession, even if it was located on the West Coast.

A bit of trivia… Chatsworth Street was supposed to be called "Ben Porter Avenue" in honor of the land's previous owners. The name didn't stick. Some would argue, thankfully. Did Barber name the street? Uncertainty reigns…

WILLIAM BOOTH BARBER AND HIS SALES SIGN

BENJAMIN F. PORTER

———————————

Roger is another member of the gang. He lives on Lahey Street in what's called Porter Ranch. Roger has a curious past, all above suspicion. He was a certified high school history teacher and a law graduate before entering the "head-hunting" business. In all things related to finance and industry, and occasional legal questions, he's the guy the group turns to. One other thing… Roger always arrives with one or more copies of the *Wall Street Journal*, the holy publication of the capitalistic world. Where possible, he leaves a copy for the Old Guy, who claims to be a very conservative Socialist. In exchange, a copy of *Mother Jones* is graciously given to Roger to challenge his political views. Both, the Old Guy believed, wanted to know what the other guy was thinking.

Now… In its original Gaelic form, Lahey means "heroic." It is the Anglicized form of the Irish surname "O Laocdha," which means "descendant of Laocdha." Laochdha is also a personal name derived from the word "laoch," meaning "hero." The name came with thousands of Irish immigrants who flooded to the New World because of the Great Potato Famine in the 1840s. That episode in Irish history, from 1845 to 1852, was known as the Great Hunger, a period of widespread starvation. The culprit was a potato blight that destroyed this staple of Irish life. At least a million people died. Millions of others left the country, with some heading to Australia and many more to America. They brought with them a motto of Irish salvation and survival: "All comes from God…" In Latin, "Tout vient de Dieu."

TIME OF HUNGER

––––––––––––––

Greg lived on Pesaro Way in Porter Ranch, a gated community north of the Old Guy's home. Greg was a founding member of the Old Guys group. Indeed, it was his efforts to start the group by recruiting his friends in the area. He was also a taskmaster. He wanted everyone, as their first assignment, to read a book entitled *The Believing Brain* and discuss various chapters at each meeting. As a former high school physics teacher at Granada Hills School, he kept everyone on their toes. His efforts were orchestrated. He wanted to move everyone toward his atheistic philosophy and a world based on rationality rather than mythology and the world of metaphysics. The Old Guys Group owes a substantial debt to Greg.

As to Pesaro Way… Now what could that name possibly mean? The exact definition was difficult to determine. However, there is a port city and resort in the Marche region of Italy near the Adriatic Sea called Pesaro. The Romans established Pesaro in 184 B.C. It was known then as Pisaurum. Modern Pesaro is known as the "Cycling City" due to its extensive network of bicycle paths. It is also known as the "City of Music," since it was the birthplace of composer Gioachino Rossini.

This leaves us with a question. Did those who named Pesaro Way know about this Italian city's history? Again, there is no clear answer to that question.

THE CITY AND ITS MUSICAL HERITAGE OF ROSSINI

Paolo lives on Kingsbury Street. He is of Italian extraction. He is also our resident scholar on all things Italian and many things European. He spent a lifetime in the restaurant business, owning his own place for years. That turned out to be important for the Old Guys meetings. Each week, one member hosts and provides bagels, lox, a pastry, and, of course, coffee. When meetings are at Paolo's place, everyone knows they are in store for a treat, something special and always delightful.

Getting back to Paolo's street, Kingsbury... It is an old Anglo-Saxon name associated with a Parish called KingsBerry (Kingsbury) in the county of Middlesex, England. The surname means "the King's Castle" or the "King's Fortress." That in turn is derived from the Old English words "cyning " (king) and "burh" (fortress). In more popular jargon, this refers to a settlement belonging to a king, which typically includes a fortified manor house or stronghold located in the counties of Middlesex, Warwickshire, or Somerset. Apparently, the Kingsbury family and their descendants lived in the area.

Their surname is first found in Hertfordshire, where John de Kingsberi was listed in the Curia Regis Rolls of 1211. The family motto was Prudens et innoccuus or "wise and innocent." That works well with Paolo; he's that guy. Obviously, all this was known when Kingsbury Street was named, or so it is assumed. One thing is for sure. The street wasn't named after a beer.

The Old Guys have another buddy on Kingsbury Street. That's Terry Roberts, who was a member, almost from the beginning of the group. Terry always brought a charming visage to the meeting, accompanied by a keen and questing mind. For years, he toiled as a Probation Officer in Los Angeles, dealing with troubled juveniles. Not an easy job. Terry, it should be noted, was (and continues to be) deeply into Buddhism and the benefits of meditation, especially for those dealing with physical pain. Due to some family obligations, he will be unable to attend our meetings. He is missed.

THE BUDDHA

———————————————

Glenn is no longer with us. He lived on Chatsworth Street and was an early member of the Old Guys. Glenn spent a lifetime in the insurance industry. He was the go-to guy when it came to how insurance policies worked (or didn't). The Old Guy would pick Glenn up around 9:00 a.m. every Tuesday. They then headed to the Western Bagel store at Balboa and San Fernando. Once there, Glenn would order a baker's dozen and a large container of cream cheese. He did this while flirting with the female staff in fluent Spanish. On the way to someone's house, the car always smelled so great. Newly baked and very warm bagels can have that effect. They always arrived by 9:30, right on time.

———————————————

Walt was an original member of the Old Guys. He always brought an assertive, New York City style to the meetings. This Vietnam vet had a sharp mind and a sharper tone when arguing a position. All remembered his oft-quoted declaration, "Think out of the box!" He did so and helped others to look beyond "the political obvious." We do miss his presence.

Walt lived on Marion Street in Porter Ranch. Who named the street, and what does it mean? Unfortunately, there's no clear answer to either question. There is Marion Avenue in Angelino Heights, but it doesn't seem to be related to the street in the Valley. Apparently, Marion is a gender-neutral French name that can mean the "star of the sea," or "beloved." The name has roots in the Hebrew, where it can mean either "bitter, or from the sea." The name is traditionally considered a girl's name. So where does that leave us? One possibility… Marion is the name of a town in several states, including Iowa, Ohio, Indiana, and Illinois. Did a civil servant for Los Angeles migrate from the Midwest and could name a street? Only conjecture, of course.

Wouldn't it be nice if street names could be changed on a whim? What a difference it would make if Marion were altered ever so slightly to Marian. Now the street sign would honor the *Music Man* and those wonderful lyrics:

Marian, Madam Librarian
What can I do, dear, to catch your ear
I love you madly, Madam Librarian, Marian
Heaven help us if the library were to catch on fire...

————————————

A Personal Note

I've never been a joiner. You know... Joining the guys for a porker game, rolling a bowling ball in a guy's league, or playing on the local softball team. No, that wasn't me. I was a bit of a lone wolf, reading my books, trying to write a bit, but certainly not out there indulging male communal companionship. And then Greg invited me to join the Old Guys. With some degree of reluctance, I did. It was one of the best decisions I ever made. I found myself enjoying the guys. Meeting with them was stimulating. In time, it became more than that. Respect and affection merged, and I formed a bond with the guys. They became an integral part of my life in ways I couldn't fully appreciate when I joined. In particular, they were there for me when Jan (my wife) was diagnosed with cancer. Quietly and steadfastly, they supported me. At that time, they became family.

CHAPTER 4 – THE REST OF THE GUYS

Jeff lives on Jovan Street. He is the cheerleader in the group for those with a strongly progressive view of the world's political landscape. Always loaded with facts buried in his ubiquitous old notebook or armed with newly cut items from a newspaper or magazine, he articulates his firmly held views with reason, passion, and, at times, elegance. It's always a treat to hear him take on the authoritarian political trends in our society.

Jeff graduated from USC's School of Pharmacy and worked for years for the State of California. He's the guy the group turns to for pharmaceutical products and other issues related to the medical industry.

Now, what about Jovan Street?

Jovan isn't a word that people banter around every day. What could it mean? It is a Slavic name that means, "God is gracious" or "sky father." In Spanish, the name Jovan is derived from the name John or Juan. In Latin, it is a variant of Jove. Jove is derived from Jupiter, which also means "Sky Father." That works since Jupiter was the supreme deity in Roman mythology, akin to the Greek Zeus, who ruled over Mount Olympus. Both deities were the gods of thunder and lightning, as well as law and order. Jovan is also associated with Christianity, particularly with John the Baptist, a significant figure in the New Testament.

In the name Jovan Street, someone had to be aware of all this. Was it some unknown civil servants working for the city? Most probably…

JUPITER, JOHN AND JESUS

One member of the Old Guys group is no longer with us. That's Norman, who almost made it to 100 years. Highly respected and adorned with affection, Norman was a long-time mainstay in the Old Guys.

For many years, Norman worked for the City of Los Angeles, beginning with the Department of Water and Power. As a Caltech engineering graduate, that was a perfect spot for Norman. Over time, he transitioned more directly into city government, serving as an advisor to the mayor's office. In this non-political role, he rose to be the highest-paid, non-elected individual in the city.

It should be noted that Norman was our Renaissance guy. Whether making stained glass windows, indulging in sculpture, or growing a vast assortment of flowers and plants, he seemed to do these things easily. And, of course, on the tennis court or the golf links, he was a forceful competitor. In senior competitions, he always did well.

Norman lived on Noble Avenue, which, in many ways, was fitting. The word suggests belonging to a hereditary class with high social or political status, perhaps even to an aristocratic one. However, the word can also describe a person, highlight fine personality traits, or uphold high moral principles and ideals. To be noble means having an unselfish character and the courage of one's convictions. An honorable person... An admired person...

And that was Norman, especially when it came to the issues of nuclear weapons and intercontinental missiles, both of which he detested with every fiber of his being. Sad to say that the struggle continues to this day to eliminate weapons of mass destruction.

NUCLEAR WEAPONS

———————————

Art lives on Vickiview Drive in West Hills. A graduate of the University of Oklahoma and a long-time physics instructor at both high school and community college levels, Art spent a lifetime nurturing budding minds with a science inclination. He brings a sober, thoughtful mind to discussions, particularly those related to Israel and the Middle East. And... He's also a strong tennis player.

Disconnecting Vicki from view, what do we have? Vicki is short for Victoria. In Latin, Victoria means victory, triumph, and success. It can also refer to a conqueror. Vicki is related to the Roman goddess of victory, Victoria. She is depicted with wings and carrying trophies of her victories. She is equivalent to the Greek Nike, goddess of victory in war and peace, who rewarded soldiers for their successful campaigns. It also provided an interesting name for tennis shoes.

VICTORIA, NIKE

———————

Al Cohen lives on Vercelli Way. For many years, he attended meetings with a sharp wit and a probing mind. However, due to some medical concerns, he can't attend now, but it's hoped that he will be able to in the future. As to the naming of his street…

Vercelli is an ancient city in the Piedmont region of northwest Italy, one of Italy's 20 regions. It was founded in 600 B.C. as an ancient Ligurian town and later a Roman city. Vercelli is renowned for its magnificent library of manuscripts, including the Codex Vercellenis, which dates to the 10th century. This book is one of the four Old English Poetic Codices. The others include the Janius manuscript in the Bodleian Library, the Exeter Book in the Exeter Cathedral Library, and the Nowell Codex in the British Library.

So where did the name come from? Perhaps from the Celtic people in a variation of the Teutonic language? Where means "station, guard, or defense." The word Cel means Celts. The union of the two words, which later became Vercelli, means "Guard station or defense of the Celts." The city itself is home to numerous Roman-era relics, including a hippodrome, an amphitheater, and a sarcophagus. Additionally, the city is also known as the "European rice capital." Who would have known?

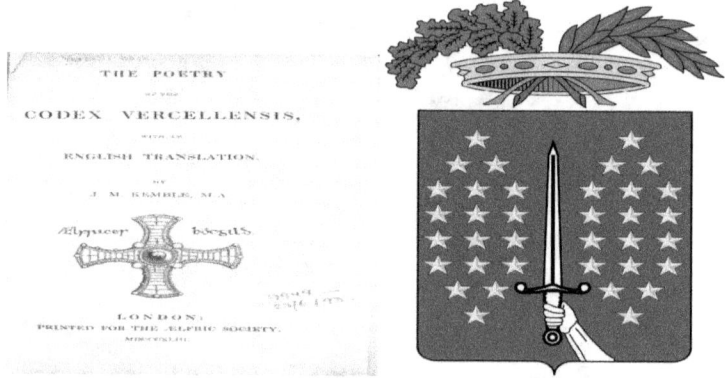

THE CODEX, THE CITY SHEILD

—————————————————

The newest member is Elliot Schneider. He brings a lively sense of history and remains well-informed about current affairs. Great to have him in this gang… Elliot was in the plumbing supply business. He lives on Index Street, a street that refers to a variety of things. It can be an indicator, sign, or measurement of something. It can be a record of names and subjects. In a basic sense, an index is a list of items in a printed book that provides the page number where something can be found. Typically, it is presented in alphabetical order. If you play the stock market, it can note a measurement of your investment's performance, or simply how Dow-Jones is doing.

The word index comes from the Latin word "indicare," which meant to point out or to indicate. The plural of the word is indices. The use of the word goes back to Greco-Roman antiquity. For those interested in trivia, the first recorded use of the word in English dates back to 1561. Whether those who named Elliot's street were aware of all this is open to conjecture.

One of the earliest uses of the term was in Plutarch's Parallel Lives, found in Sir Thomas North's 1595 translation. A close second was Henry Scobell's *Acts and Ordinances of Parliament,* published in 1658.

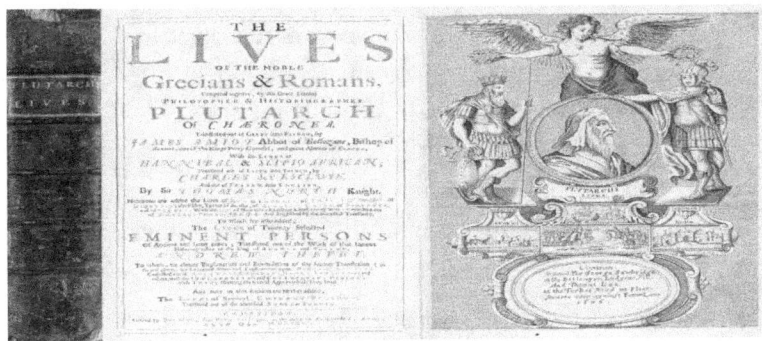

THE TRANSLATION, SIR THOMAS NORTH

Mark Sherman lives on Beckford Street in Porter Ranch. He's our medical expert, having worked as an anesthesiologist for Kaiser Medical for years. While he administered anesthesia and pain medication during surgery he never puts the Old Guys to sleep, not with his sharp, to-the-point comments.

As to the origin and meaning of Beckford Street… It is an English surname. It comes from a locale in Worcestershire, England. The word is derived from the Middle English word "Becke" and the Old English word "ford." That's close to another Old English term, "becca," which means a stream or ford. It indeed refers to a place where a river may be forced by wading. Was an anonymous civil servant aware of this history, or perhaps the subdivision developer? Difficult to know for sure…

So, there you have it—Old Guys living in the San Fernando Valley on streets with a variety of names, hopefully no longer a mystery as to what they mean. Having pulled together these strands of history, it was time to move on. The Old Guy knew that.

CHAPTER 5 – NAMING STREETS

Naming a street is not a haphazard undertaking. Urban planners and housing developers are responsible for naming streets in new neighborhoods and changing old names if necessary. In doing so, they adhere to specific general guidelines. For example:

(1) A street name shall not contain more than 18 letters. (So much for Robert K. Livingston Way)

(2) Similar-sounding names are to be avoided within the same fire-fighting district or postal zone to eliminate identification problems. (By way of example: Sesnon Boulevard in Granada Hills and Severance Street in University Park)

(3) Names must be unambiguous. (Does Hartsook Street meet this requirement?)

(4) A new street name should be different from any name already in use in a specific area. (Do Woodley Avenue and Woodman Avenue meet this test?)

(5) The name shouldn't be difficult to pronounce. (Vose and Lull Streets meet that demand, but what about Wyandotte Street?)

(6) Streets are not named after any commercial organization or to honor a living person. (Vinnie of Dodger fame comes to mind)

(7) Historic names may refer to "applicable geographical features" whenever possible. (Granada Hills and Mission Hills by way of example)

(8) Names may be chosen because of certain traits planners want people to associate with a new area. (Go Santa Anita Avenue)

Those are the guidelines. Obviously, and sometimes confusingly, there can be exceptions to the rules. They, however, represent a rational way to name streets. However, this can lead to confusion. How often have you answered the question, "What Street do you live on?" Quite usually, I'm sure. You probably responded, "Hey, I live on Woodman." But wait. That street is an avenue. Or try this one on for size. "I live on Brand." Sounds okay except that this street is a "boulevard." I want another challenge. "I live on Sherman Way." Sounds fine, but… What's a "way" compared to a "lane" or "drive?" I think you can see where this is going. We need definitions and examples to clarify what a street is in the naming process. In other words, a street is a street by a variety of different names.

Let's begin with the term road. Very simply, it is a public way connecting two or more areas. Therefore, every street is a road. However, a street differs from a road in that it is a public way at least 40 feet wide, permitting both pedestrian and vehicular traffic access to various locations. One example of a street is Oxnard Street, named after the town of Oxnard in Ventura County but located in the San Fernando Valley. Obviously, there's a story here, as there is with every street sign throughout the Valley.

The town of Oxnard and the street were named after Henry T. Oxnard, a French American industrialist (1860-1922) who ran the American Beet Sugar Company. Growing sugar beets was a significant business in Ventura and the San Fernando Valley at one time. Oxnard established sugar refineries in Chino in 1891 and in Rancho Colonia, just south of the City of Ventura, in 1898. Over time, Rancho Colonia evolved into the city of Oxnard.

How did that happen? Initially, Henry T. wanted to name the town "Sakchar," Greek for "sugar." When dealing with the folks in Sacramento by phone, a problem arose. They couldn't understand what he was saying. In exasperation, he finally yelled, "Just name the place after me!" They did. As it turns out, several streets in the Valley were borrowed from Ventura County, including Saticoy and Nordhoff. One last thing… Oxnard Street is relevant to sugar beets, as approximately 15,000 acres were used for that crop in the San Fernando Valley. The harvest was shipped to Oxnard for processing. How about that!

THE VENTURA FACTORY, HENRY T. OXNARD

What is an avenue? Essentially, it is a broad public street lined with charming trees on either side, making it visually appealing. An avenue almost always goes north-south, unlike a street that generally goes east-west. An avenue tends to be wide and is sometimes called a thoroughfare. For example…

Woodman Avenue is named after Frederic Thomas Woodman (1872-1945), who was once Los Angeles' mayor during a three-year stint. Woodman's home state was New Hampshire, where he practiced law. He came to the City of Angels in 1907. In time, he entered the city government, most notably as harbor commissioner. He championed developing San Pedro as the port of Los Angeles.

The harbor, as you might know, was named San Pedro in honor of St. Peter of Alexandria, whose feast day is November 24th, as determined by the ecclesiastical calendar of Spain. That was also the day that Juan Rodriguez Cabrillo (1499-1543) first explored San Pedro Bay in 1542. In 1784, San Pedro emerged as a town. In that year, Spain deeded Rancho San Pedro to Juan Jose Dominguez. (1736-1809) The land grant gave him control of over 75,000 acres. It was also the first land grant in Alta California. Dominguez, a retired soldier, was honored for his work in assisting the Portola expedition in 1769-1770, and got all that?

FREDERIC T. WOODMAN, JUAN RODRIGUEZ
CABRILLO, JUAN JOSE DOMIGUEZ

By way of another example, the street named Zelzah Avenue has a curious background. It is one of the very few biblical street names in Los Angeles. It is a Hebrew word meaning "shadow" or "clear shade." It can also be referred to as a place protecting from the sun, a place of shade. The word appears only once in the Old Testament, in the First Book of Samuel. There is a meeting between two men at "Rachel's tomb at Zelzah. Here things get complicated. Zelzah might also refer to a suburb of Jerusalem, to an oasis, or to the hour of high noon. Given that, how did it become a street name?

It was the original name of Northridge, California, from 1910 to 1929, when the town was primarily a rail depot. Emily Vose Wright (1855-1917) named the area. She was the wife of Francis Marion "Bud" Wright. (1841-1937) He sold the Hubbard and Wright ranch in 1909 for development, some 1,100-prime grain-raising acres to the Valley Farm Company for subdivision. In time, it would be the future site of Northridge. The ranch had been referred to as Zelzah, as was the family's home in the City of San Fernando.

A word about land transfer... Wright had owned the land with Henry Hubbard. (1844-1929) Does Hubbard's name sound familiar? It should. It's a street located in Sylmar, California, for the most part, and in the town of San Fernando. Wright and Hubbard bought the land from Benjamin Porter in 1887. Porter once owned the land with Charles Maclay and a relative, George K. Porter. They had purchased the land from the heirs of Eulogio de Celis, a Spaniard who bought the Ex-Mission de San Fernando from the Mexican government for $14,000 in 1846. Wow! Real estate deals on steroids...

A word about Emily Vose Wright... Besides being married to "Bud," she was an early schoolteacher in the City of San Fernando from 1877 to 1886. In addition to teaching schoolchildren and working on the ranch, she was a staunch prohibitionist who fought to keep San Fernando dry. It is unclear what her husband's views were on this subject. In any event, Emily has a street named after her—Vose Street, located here in the San Fernando Valley.

EMILY VOSE WRIGHT, CHARLES MACLAY, HENRY C. HUBBARD

What is a boulevard? It is generally understood to be a broad paved public way at least 200 feet wide. In many cases, trees are grown on both sides of the street. The name comes from the French word "allee," which means to "arrive or to come to." In Spanish, the word is "alameda." Three boulevards in the San Fernando Valley quickly come to mind: Brand, Sepulveda, and Los Feliz.

Brand Boulevard was named after Leslie Coombs Brand (1859-1925). He was a streetcar magnate and developer. He is credited with being the "father of Glendale, California. He subdivided what is now called Mission Hills and connected it to Los Angeles with a streetcar line. Today's Brand Boulevard follows the route of its original car line. A charming story is about Brand. He was involved in the naming of Maryland Avenue in Glendale. One of his truck managers had a daughter named Mary. She was engaged to a man named Land. The two names were combined to create Maryland Avenue. That's a pretty nice boss to do that.

Los Feliz Boulevard was named in 1888 after Rancho Los Feliz, which was a Spanish land grant issued to Captain Jose Vicente Feliz. (1741-1822) He had led the expedition to what became the Pueblo of Los Angeles (El Pueblo de Nuestra Señora la Reina de Los Ángeles). In everyday English, that translates to "the town of the Queen of Angels." The expedition brought 11 families from Sonora, Mexico, in 1781. Much of the land was in the Silver Lake area and on the higher slopes of what is now Griffith Park. As a point of interest… Two varieties of trees were planted on the boulevard: Cedrus Atlantica and Cedrus Dedara. This was done in 1935 as a joint beautification project of the Los Feliz Improvement Association and the Los Feliz Women's Club. The trees are still there.

LESLIE C. BRAND, NO TRAFFIC

The name Sepulveda refers to a distinguished Spanish family led by Patriarch Francisco Xavier Sepulveda (1747-1788). He was a Mexican-born soldier in the Spanish army who arrived in Alta, California, in 1781. As was the custom in his day, his successful military exploits and valor provided many perks, including, in his case, land grants deeded by the Spanish authorities. His land holdings would encompass a significant portion of what high-priced real estate is today, including Palos Verdes, San Pedro, and Santa Monica. His ranch was called Rancho San Vicente y Santa Monica. Now that's a perk.

Some more trivia... The Portola expedition of 1769-1770 was in the Los Angeles area, seeking a way to reach and follow the coastline. Led by Gaspar de Portola (1716-1786), the expedition encountered steep coastal cliffs in the Pacific Palisades area. The topography challenged the party. Undaunted by this, they turned inland. In doing so, they found a pass through the Santa Monica Mountains, which brought them to the San Fernando Valley. This was the first recorded European exploration of the interior of present-day California. Initially, the pass had been a faint footpath used by the Tongva, an indigenous people. They had as many as 100 villages in Southern California and the Channel Islands. In all, the expedition found an overland route from Baja California to Monterey and San Francisco.

A bit more about Sepulveda Boulevard… It was once considered the longest surface street in L.A. County. The road was shortened in 2018 when El Segundo made a two-mile stretch through their area, a part of the Pacific Coast Highway. Also… It was initially known as Military Avenue when it was in the West L.A. area. In 1925, the name was changed to its current marker. About ten years later, the boulevard was extended through the Santa Monica Mountains via the Sepulveda Pass, which had been renamed earlier in 1922 to connect with the former Saugus Avenue in the Valley. That street was named in 1916 and once extended northward into the San Fernando Valley.

Saugus is a Native American word, but not from any California group. It is an Algonquin word translated as "great, outlet, or extended." Henry Mayo Newhall (1825-1882), born in Saugus, Maine, and owner of over 46,000 acres in the Santa Clarita Valley, gave that name to the original Saugus Road. That was in 1888. Of course, the town of Newhall was named after this expatriate from the Atlantic Coast. Newhall was, it should be pointed out, originally a railroad depot.

GASPAR DE PORTOLA, THE EXPEDITION

HENRY M. NEWHALL SEPULVEDA PASS
NEWHALL RAILROAD DEPOT

ALL STREETS WITH A HISTORY…

CHAPTER 6 – OTHER STREET NAMES

It is time to move on to another name for a street, in this case, a court. Specifically, it is a rectangular pocket off a public way. It is sometimes known as a "dead-end" street that ends in a loop or circle (cul-de-sac). Examples abound.

Dale Court and Trigger Street were named after two Chatsworth celebrities. You are certainly aware of them. Dale Evans (1912-2001) was a Western singer and actress in the Roy Rogers (1911-1996) movies. She was also Roger's wife. Trigger was Rogers' beautiful palomino horse. Together, they thrilled a generation of youngsters, who left the movie theater wanting to shoot straight and bring to justice the bad guys in dark hats and darker mustaches.

ROY AND DALE, TRIGGER

Pacoima Court in Studio City is an artifact of a sort. Before 1923, a long stretch of Laurel Canyon Boulevard across the San Fernando Valley was known as Pacoima Avenue, as it led to Pacoima. Pacoima Avenue was renamed Laurel Canyon in 1929, leaving one little street behind as a memento to the area's past --- Pacoima Court. The name Pacoima is derived from the indigenous people in this region. As to Laurel Canyon...

It takes its name from the California bay laurel, which once grew wild in the area. Laurel means the same thing in Spanish. It was definitely not named after Stan Laurel, the comedic actor in the classic black-and-white Laurel and Hardy films.

LAUREL AND HARDY

Laker/Celtic Court is located in Chatsworth, California. The name was notarized on June 5, 1987, on land owned by Theodore O. Stein, Jr., during the NBA Finals between the LA Lakers and the Boston Celtics. The name of the two cul-de-sacs was not a coincidence. Celtic Court was once known as Celtic Street. Stein, it appears, had some sway in City Hall. He served as both the airport and harbor commissioners. He pushed for a name change. The Lakers won the series four-2. Go Lakers… Go Kareem… Go Magic…

Another name for a street is a drive. It is often described as a recreational or scenic way, perhaps through a park. Usually, it is a long road that winds around a geographical feature such as a lake, river, or mountain. It can also be a very short street.

One unfamiliar drive is named after a very familiar aerospace company: Lockheed Corporation. The story begins on September 14, 1971. Robert A. Swanson was the mayor of Burbank. He wanted to honor the company for its contributions to the City of Burbank by naming a street after it. With this in mind, he hosted breakfast at the famous Castaway restaurant. There, he announced his plans to establish a "Lockheed lookout point" in the Starlight Bowl's parking lot and to name a road leading into the lot, Lockheed Drive. That didn't work. Burbank already had a Lockheed Drive at the airport. Since that was the case, the mayor changed the name slightly to Lockheed View Drive. It should be noted that the street offered no view of any Lockheed facility. Oh, well...

MAYOR SWANSON

Marbro Drive is in Encino. This cul-de-sac was not named for the Marx Brothers, no matter how hard you try to bring "Mar" and "Bro" together. Though it's confusing, a drive can also be a "dead end." The street was named for Leonard Gayle Mark (1917-1999) and Melvin "Mel" Mark (1914-1991), who came to L.A. in the 1920s after living in Omaha, Nebraska. Now this leads to a conclusion. "Mar" refers to a last name. "Bro" refers to the two brothers. Their father was Abraham Mark. He was the city's health commissioner before finding greater financial rewards in real estate. This led the family to establish the Marbro Development Company, which built and sold properties in the San Fernando Valley from the 1950s through the 1970s. Recall that developers can suggest names for new streets. And one more thing... The street name has nothing to do with the cigarette brand or a tough-as-leather cowboy.

Those who live in the Valley are very familiar with Mulholland Drive. Most people know it's named after William Mulholland (1855-1935), and, like him or not, they have a glass of water to thank for his L.A. history. It all began when he left Belfast, Ireland, at the age of 15, finally settling in our city in 1877. In 1902, the town formed the Water Department, the forerunner to the present Department of Water and Power. Mulholland became the first superintendent of the agency. And this is when things get feisty. He argued for and eventually helped build the Los Angeles Aqueduct Project, which brought water from the Owens Valley in the Eastern Sierra Mountains. Though the farmers were unhappy with this, the project was completed in 1913. A bitter struggle between the Owens Valley farmers and Los Angeles continues to this day.

Trouble Again Breaks Out In Owens Valley-Los Angeles Bitter Water Fight

The completed aqueduct brought water not only to thirsty L.A. but also to the semi-arid San Fernando Valley and farmers in the southland. Mullholland also had a hand in constructing Lake Hollywood by flooding Weid Canyon with the Mulholland Dam. Mulholland also considered a hilltop highway, which was eventually built and named after him. It was opened in 1924, financed by a consortium of developers investing in the Hollywood Hills. DeWitt Reaburn was the construction engineer responsible for constructing the road. As it was being built, he claimed: "The Mulholland Highway is destined to be one of the heaviest traveled and one of the best-known scenic roads in the U.S." That seems to be the case.

THE BUILDER AND THE PIPELINE

WATER FOR THE SAN FERNANDO VALLEY

Of course, the most famous drive, some would argue, isn't really in the Valley. It's in Beverly Hills. Rodeo Drive was once part of the massive Rancho Rodeo de las Aguas. The name meant the "gathering of the waters." Initially, the land was granted to Maria Rita Valdez Villa. (1791-1854) She owned approximately 3,200 acres. Her ranch had cattle, sheep, pigs, sugar beets, and barley. Her adobe was located at today's corner of Alpine Street and Sunset Boulevard/ In later years, the land changed hands. The Rodeo Land and Water Company took possession. Burton E. Green was the company's head. (1868-1965) He hoped to find liquid gold. That is, oil. He didn't. Instead, he built the subdivision that is now known as Beverly Hills, California. Its main street is Rodeo Drive.

BURTON GREEN, THE FAMOUS STREET

Another name for a street is lane. Now, what does that suggest? A lane is a narrow, informal street or passageway. It does not have a median. Here's an example. Edward Everett Horton Lane is in Encino, California. It is named after the character actor. You might remember him in the classic, *Lost Horizon*, where he played the role of an English archaeologist and reluctant resident of Shangri-La. For a time, he served as the community's honorary mayor. That worked since he owned an 18-acre ranch in Encino.

In retirement, he used his voice as the narrator of the Saturday/Sunday morning Bullwinkle cartoon --- "Fractured Fairy Tales."

THE VOICE, THE SHOW

Scadlock Lane is in Sherman Oaks, a lovely area that one might really call Sherwood Forest. Want to know more? Of course you do. The street was named after Will Scadlock, who is called "Will Scadlock" in the story of Robin Hood. Will was one of the merry men in that tale. The street name came from two brothers, Milton and Bert Klein, who owned the Sherwood Park Investment Company. In planning their subdivision, they used numerous names with which Robin's followers are familiar, including Longbow Drive, Woodcliff, Deerhorn Road, and Shernoll Court. The brothers, however, did not see a street after the nasty Sheriff of Nottingham and his even nastier boss, the infamous Prince John.

ROBIN HOOD IN SHERWOOD FOREST

Check out these photos, a bandleader and a family of singers. What could they have to do with street signs?

THE SINGERS, THE BAND LEADER
READING LEFT TO RIGHT, ROSEMARY, PORISCILLA,
GALE AND LOLA

Using the word 'lane' in a street name can reveal some fascinating history. For example, the Lane sisters were from Iowa, four girls who got a big break in 1933 when they sang for Fred Waring (1900-1984) and his band. This led to roles in a series of movies. Priscilla was in Alfred Hitchcock's *Saboteur* and *Arsenic and Old Lace*. Priscilla Lane is named in her honor. Legend has it that she broke a champagne bottle over the street sign when it was christened in 1941. Less than a mile away is Rosemary Lane, which is named after Priscilla's big sister. Another sister found a degree of fame in a uniquely unusual way. Her name was Lola. Sadly, no street was named for her. However, Jerry Siegel, the co-creator of Superman, named Lois Lane after Lola. So, there you go.

The term "way" is another way to describe a street. Talk about a poor play on words. A way is a narrow road. It can be a small side street connected to a larger road. Though it is not precisely in the center of the San Fernando Valley, General Thaddeus Kosciuszko Way has a fascinating history. It is a two-block access road laid out in 1871. That was during the redevelopment of Bunker Hill. It was called 2nd Place, not a very appealing name. In 1976, the L.A. The City Council was requested to change the name. Who was behind this?

That turned out to be Mary Dziadula (1846-1917), who lived in Burbank. She wanted General Kosciuszko to be honored for his services during the Revolutionary War. This former Polish army officer assisted in building fortifications for the Continental Army. At first, the powers-that-be denied her request. The name was too long to be on a street sign. People would have trouble spelling and pronouncing the name. Apparently, she was persistent. In January 1978, the City Council approved the name, and Mary was delighted. I guess that amounts to Polish pride. Kosciuszko found a home.

THE GENERAL, THE SINGER

Street names can be misleading. For example, it wouldn't be uncommon for folks to equate Graceland Way with Elvis Presley. Of course, that wasn't the case. Located in Glendale, Graceland Way was named after Grace Farrar, the wife of Bert Farrar and the force behind the development of Chevy Chase. That development was not named after Chevy Chase, despite what you may think. That actor's real name was Cornelius Crane Chase. Now, I am getting back to Grace's husband. You develop the subdivision and get some naming rights, as we've seen before. Now to confuse things a bit… Grace was originally from Iowa. Before marriage, her name was Grace E. Laird. As it turns out, there's a small cul-de-sac near Chevy Chase Drive called Laird Drive. How about that?

A Personal Note

"For many years, I thought Sherman Way was named after the Union general, William Tecumseh. Sherman (1820-1891). He did pave the way to Atlanta. He did help the Union's cause. As a history teacher, I was aware of that. But boy was I wrong about that street sign. Proves again that assumptions can lead you astray. Still, it would not have been a misplaced honor had the street been named after the General. As one unknown poet said:

Still onward we pressed, till our banners
Swept out from Atlanta's grim walls,
And the blood of the patriot dampened
The sol where the traitor-flag falls;
We [did not] weep for the fallen,
Who slept by each river and tree,
Yet we twined them a wreath of laurel,
As Sherman marched down to the sea.

The original Sherman Way was the Valley's first thoroughfare. In 1926, the street was renamed Van Nuys Blvd. In the same year, another street, East Sherman Way (an entirely separate street), was renamed Chandler Boulevard. While this was happening, West Sherman Way (another separate street) became the Sherman Way we know today. A year later, the Sherman Oaks subdivision was dedicated. Now, as to whom Sherman Way was named... Confusing.

Moses Hazeltine Sherman (1853-1932) was a big name in the development of Los Angeles. Originally from a farming community in

Vermont, he moved first to Arizona before coming to L.A. There, he went into the railroad business to connect somewhat distant suburbs, including Santa Monica, Pasadena, and Hollywood. That was in 1896. His company, it should be noted, required an area to house its workers and to establish a rail yard. Naturally, he called it "Sherman." Why not? He was the boss. Eventually, the town became known as West Hollywood. Years later, he sold his railroad interests to seek a greater fortune in real estate. He was involved in the development of Playa del Rey. He was also tied to another development known as Hollywoodland (which gave us the iconic Hollywood sign).

And one more thing… Much of the land he developed was purchased from Isaac Van Nuys (1835-1912) in 1909. Isaac, as you know, also has a street named after him. Before we leave Sherman… He had a daughter whom he named Hazeltine. Apparently, he called a street after her, or perhaps for his whole family. This point is somewhat unclear.

MOSES HAZELTINE SHERMAN, THE ORIGINAL SIGN

GENERAL SHERMAN

––––––––––––––––––––

A Personal Note

So, there you have it. Streets can be called by almost any name (within the rules), and the type of street varies from a lane to a drive, to a boulevard, to an avenue, to a way, to a road, and to a street. That said, an aside… I was raised in San Francisco. My home address was 8-7ᵗʰ Avenue in the Richmond District, adjacent to the Presidio and Mountain Lake Park. However, citizens of the City of Saint Francis referred to the street (my avenue) as the "block." Go figure.

––––––––––––––––

It was time to move on. The Old Guy had bigger fish to fry.

CHAPTER 7 – THE MAP

The San Fernando Valley is a vast piece of sprawling real estate encompassing 345 square miles. That's about eight times the size of Manhattan. Sorry, New York, you're not that big an apple." Located within this expanse are numerous suburban residential communities, including Northridge, Porter Ranch, Chatsworth, Encino, Van Nuys, and Woodland Hills. Not to be unnoticed are such enclaves as Tarzana, Canoga Park, Winnetka, and the "hill" spots --- Mission Hills, Granada Hills, and North Hills. Additionally, there are communities with a distinct Spanish heritage, including Sylmar, San Fernando, and Pacoima. Check the map below. It helps in identifying areas and their locations in the Valley.

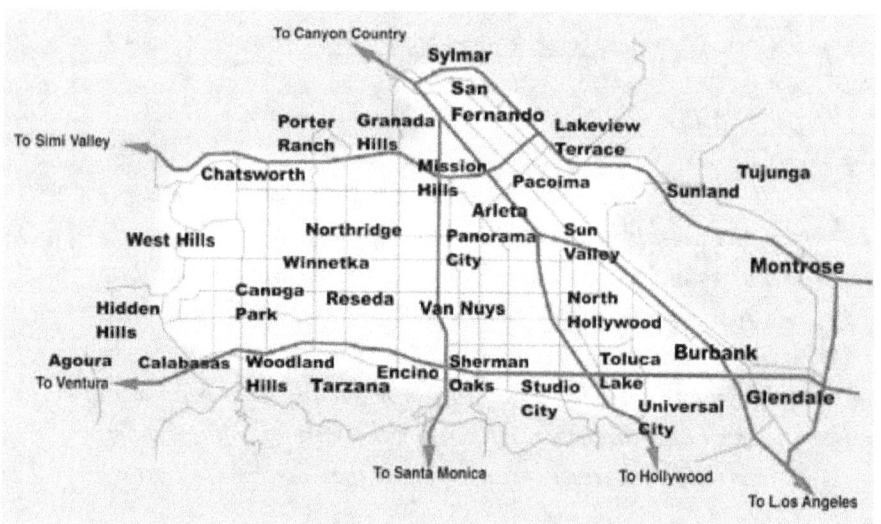

THE SAN FERNANDO VALLEY

Lots of land… Lots of postal zones… Lots of diverse communities… And lots of street signs…

Behind every name on the map lies a history, usually beginning with the Spanish expeditions into the area and continuing later with the Valley's Mexican heritage before the Yankees moved in on a large scale. Within each community, there are numerous signs indicating street names. It is difficult to give a precise number of city streets named in the San Fernando Valley. That's because there are multiple cities in the Valley, including Burbank, Glendale, San Fernando, Calabasas, Hidden Hills, Panorama City, and, of course, other areas of the Valley eventually annexed by the City of Los Angeles.

Each city has its own street naming history. Naturally, the number of streets constantly changes as new development projects emerge. Nothing is for sure. At one time, the Valley was home to indigenous people, and then Europeans arrived, all vying for land. Always the land... For the missionaries... For the farmers and ranchers... For those who extracted wealth from the land... And for those who envisioned future towns, inexorably prodded by one magic word: "subdivision." In its own way, the San Fernando Valley experienced its own form of "manifest destiny." What President John Quincy Adams (1825-1829) said long ago rang true, not only for a nation but for the SFV:

The entire continent appears destined to be occupied by a single nation. The acquisition of a definite boundary line to the Pacific forms a great epoch in our history.

Walt Whitman echoed the same sentiments poetically.

All the past we leave behind,
We debouch upon a newer, mightier world, a varied world,
Fresh and strong, the world we seize, the world of labor and the March,
Pioneers! O pioneers!

CHAPTER 8 – WIDER SPACES

Streets are found within larger locations. For example, Fullerfarm Street is located in Northridge, California. I bet you didn't know that. It was named after Percy Francis Fuller (1881-1962). He sold many one-acre plots. Buyers could live in the front and raise chickens in the back. Apparently, Fuller was something of a poultry authority, or so he claimed. I think that's called having your eggs and chickens, too.

Another street in Northridge is Citronia. The name comes from a subdivision development known as "Citronia Acres." The lots offered for sale ranged in size from 5 to 40 acres, providing ample space for a home and citrus groves. This was in January 1915. A few days after opening for business (six days later), the City of L.A. annexed the area. How's that timing? In 1921, an unnamed road in the subdivision was belatedly christened Citronia Street.

Worth their~ Weight in GOLD!

FULLER POULTRY FARMS, under the supervision of P. F. Fuller, three years poultry expert for Los Angeles' greatest milling company and recognized as California's leading poultry authority, assure owners yearly a

$2000 to $4000 Profit

No experience necessary. Come out Sunday and see the model Fuller Poultry Farm, said to be the finest ever planned for one-acre chicken ranches. Small cost to build. Talk with Mr. Fuller about POSITIVE PROFITS from chickens on **one-acre** Fuller Poultry Farms.

$1750 an Acre

Some streets run through two or more large areas. For example, Prairie Street is found in both Northridge and Chatsworth. It appears that one Frank Charles Hageman is responsible for the street name. (1870-1953). He was from Chicago, and his firm, the San Fernando Development Company, acquired the land rights to 950 acres in what is now called Chatsworth. Hageman brought with him any number of Chicago Street names he was familiar with, including Dearborn, Halsted, Kinzie, Superior, and Prairie. From the "Windy City" to the land of sunshine, so to speak.

And, of course, there is Tampa Avenue. This street tracks through Northridge, Porter Ranch, Reseda, and Tarzana. No one is quite sure how the street got its name. In 1910, the street was called Maple Avenue. Around 1917, Maple Avenue was renamed Tampa Avenue by an anonymous city engineer. There was a good reason to do this. There was a conflict between Maple Avenue in the Valley and Maple Avenue in Los Angeles. Something had to give to end the confusion. As to the name Tampa...

Was it named for the city in Florida? No one knows. Here's one theory. Tampa is like Maple—two-syllable, five-letter words that share certain letters, such as "a," "m," and "p." Still another view concerns Hernando de Soto, who visited Tampa Bay in 1639. Was Tampa chosen as a match for nearby De Soto Avenue? Hard to know...

All these streets run through Northridge and are tied to the San Fernando Valley. So how did the Valley get its name? We begin this story on September 8, 1797. On that date, a Catholic Mission was established by a Spanish priest. He did so in what is now known as the City of San Fernando. His name was Father Fry Fermin Francisco de Lasuen. In Spanish, the mission was called Mission San Fernando Rey de España. The mission was named in honor of King Ferdinand III of Castile and Leon and would be the first of seventeen settlements.

De Lasuen was following on the work of two Franciscan padres who accompanied the earlier Portola expedition of 1768. The monks were there to record the expedition's travels and discoveries, as well as to identify locations for a proposed network of missions along the royal highway in

California, known as El Camino Real (the royal road). The two monks were Junipero Serra and Juan Crespi. Their exploration carried them through the Sepulveda Pass and into the San Fernando Valley. They named the area Valle de Santa Catarina de Bononia de los Encinos (Valley of St. Cathrine of Bononia of Oaks). We've shortened that to the "Valley."

JUNÍPERO SERRA, JUAN CRESPI

As noted before, the Old Guy lived in Northridge, California, as did some of his friends. That being the case, how did Northridge get its name? To determine this, we need to go back to 1908 when settlers moved into the area and dubbed their community Zelzah. Again, that name refers to a place of shade, where the sun doesn't beat down on you. That name lasted until 1929, when Zelzah was renamed North Los Angeles. Once more, the name was temporary. There was confusion between North Hollywood and North Hollywood, not between North Hollywood and North Los Angeles. One name had to go. In 1938, Carl S. Dentzel proposed renaming the area Northridge Village. In the time that became Northridge... No future changes are planned. But you never know...

Dentzel was quite a guy (1913-1980). He had a career in journalism. During World War II, he worked to improve America's relationships with Mexico and Central and South America. He served as the Executive Secretary for the Southern California Council for Inter-American Affairs.

That led to his involvement with the Southwest Museum. He was the director for twenty-five years. He worked unceasingly to conserve the cultural heritage of Los Angeles. That effort led to the preservation of the El Pueblo de Los Angeles and to the creation of the city's Cultural Heritage Board. In her own right, his wife (Elizabeth Waldo Dentzel) was a musician and composer who emphasized intercultural music in the San Fernando Valley.

SOUTHWEST MUSEUM, THE TEAM

The history of Northridge dates back to the Tongva people, who settled in the area approximately 2,000 years ago. According to anthropologists, they lived in dome-shaped houses and have been referred to as "the people of the earth. Many of their pictographs were destroyed as the San Fernando Valley was subdivided. The Spanish period, of course, led to eventual Mexican control over the years. In 1840, the Mexican governor was Pío Pico. He sold large tracks of land to Eulogio de Celis (1845-1903). This native of Spain was noted in 1850 as an "agriculturist" with real estate holdings worth $20,000. In time, his heirs sold the northern half of their holdings to Senator George K. Porter, a land purchase that included the Northridge area. He called his holdings the "Valley of the Cumberland."

de CELIS, THE TONGVA PEOPLE

At this point, the road to Northridge begins with the Hawk Ranch, some 1,100 acres of prized land. Marion "Bud" Wright developed the ranch with the assistance of George K. Porter. In 1908, the Southern Pacific Railroad laid tracks through the Hawk Ranch, creating a "railroad boom town." The train station was located at the northeast corner of what is now Parthenia Avenue and Reseda Boulevard, just across the street from a water well. Over time, the Hawk Ranch was sold for subdivision and renamed Zelzah. This led the Scandia Land and Loan Company to advertise Zelzah Acres, with land available for $250 per acre.

The advertising would have made Madison Avenue proud: the land is "the cream of the San Fernando Valley, the richest soil in California." The company highlighted the ease of transportation due to the railroad station and the absence of alkali, adobe, or hardpan soil. It also noted that water for domestic purposes could be found at depths ranging from 35 to 65 feet, and for irrigation, at depths ranging from 140 to 300 feet. The advertising paid off. Land values increased. By 1913, E.O. Hanson and Sons were selling land at $325 an acre. Contemporary folks sure missed out on that deal. One thing is sure about Northridge and the San Fernando Valley. Land was present, but water brought from afar formed the Valley.

GUSHING WATER ARRIVES THROUGH THE PIPELINE

1913 – ONLOOKERS RELISH THE TORRENT OF WATER

THE MIRACLE OF THE VALLEY

The Valley has always been on the sharp edge of biting commentaries, perhaps because of its proximity to downtown L.A. A sort of guilt by association... Sometimes the pointed words do resonate with the Valley. Dorothy Parker quipped, by way of example, that "Los Angeles was 72 suburbs in search of a city." Billy Connolly phrased it this way: "I love Los Angeles. It reinvents itself every two days." And Frank Lloyd Wright shared this bit of affection: "Tip the world over on its side and everything loose will land in Los Angeles." Whatever the merits of these views, one thing is for sure. Water made everything possible in the land of the suburbs.

CHAPTER 9– RESEDA AND MORE

Two streets run through the next area of interest: Porter Ranch. Reseda Boulevard crosses the San Fernando Valley in a north-south pattern while Rinaldi Street traverses in an east-west fashion. Both roads are tied to the Porter Ranch area of the Valley. A word about them…

The word "Reseda" refers to Reseda odorata, the Latin name for a fragrant flower known as the mignonette. Many believe Reseda was named after the flower. When Reseda was established as a large subdivision in 1911, Reseda odorata was known for its olive-like shade of green. That color was popular in women's fashions. Perhaps, as some believe, it wasn't the plant but the color that led to the naming of Reseda.

RESEDA ODORATA

In any event, Reseda's original name was Marian. This was to honor Marian Otis Chandler. (1866-1952) She was a corporate secretary for the *Los Angeles Times*. Her father was Harrison Gray Otis (1837-1917), who was involved in the development of the Reseda subdivision. At that time, Reseda Avenue (its first name) was one of the first streets in the project. Later, the name was changed to Reseda Boulevard. It would carry traffic from the Santa Monica Mountains to the Santa Susana Mountains and Porter Ranch in the north. That's a 12-mile stretch.

MARIAN OTIS CHANDLER, HARRISON GRAY OTIS

Rinaldi Street honors a Valley pioneer. That was Carl Robert Rinaldi. His real name was Carel Ambrosus Roberto Rinaldi. Try putting that name on a street sign. His summarized background was this. He was born in Berlin. His father was Italian, and his mother was Hungarian. He arrived in the United States in the 1850s, settling in L.A. in 1859. In time, he established a flourishing upholstery store. He also married a local gal. That was Francisca Valdez. All very nice… But what does it have to do with the street? In 1872, Rinaldi sold his business and bought 150 acres near today's Van Norman Reservoir, where he farmed the land, growing oranges, grapes, and olives (well, he was Italian). At one time, he had 2,000 olive trees and was considered an expert on the plant. In 1916, the street was named after him.

CONSTRUCTING RINALDI STREET (1976)

Porter Ranch owes its beginnings to Benjamin K. Porter. In the late 19th century, he purchased a sizable portion of the Rancho-Ex Mission San Fernando, land in the foothills of the Santa Susana Mountains, just above Northridge. That amounted to a third of the northern valley. Nice purchase. Benjamin Porter's descendants held onto the area until the early 1960s. In time, ranches for cultivation and horses turned into a series of subdivisions. The post-war housing boom was on.

The Valley was a gigantic subdivision awaiting the returning members of the armed forces, all of them eligible to buy a home courtesy of the G.I. Bill. The human equation was in place: (a) get married; (b) start a family; and (c) move into a three-bedroom bungalow in the valley. What could be better? Boom times had come to the Valley. Still, the past hovered in the shadows.

In the 1700s, the Gabrielino Indians lived in the area because of a natural watering hole at present-day Reseda and Parthenia Streets. The area's first name flowed from that spring. Zelzah, you'll recall, referred to an oasis in the *Bible* and to Northridge's first name. And then time passed… Although not intentional, Steven Spielberg inadvertently brought unanticipated notoriety to Porter Ranch with his 1982 film E.T. the Extra-Terrestrial. Present-day *E.T.* Park is a reminder of that blockbuster film.

WELCOME TO PORTER RANCH

ET

"E.T.", GEORGE K. PORTER

Rinaldi Street goes through Granada Hills, California. Within that area, there are four streets with interesting backgrounds: Valjean Ave, Monogram Avenue, Cagney Street, and Sesnon Boulevard. Let's find out about them before dealing with how Granada Hills came about.

Valjean Avenue originated on the West Van Nuys tract. It opened in 1923. The promoters behind this were a local hardware merchant (Arthur Ely Streeter) and an ex-railroad guy (Rollin Coleman Smith). There is a mystery surrounding the origin of the street name. One possible theory... Perhaps the two men were thinking of Jan Valjean, the hero of Victor Hugo's novel, *Les Misérables.* Or was it named after Eugene Valjean, a civil engineer working in L.A.? Already two streets had been named after civil engineers: Lull Street and Lecouvreur Avenue. Still another possibility concerns wordplay. Did "Val" stand for "Valley?" Did "Jean" stand for Streeter's infant daughter, "Majorie Jean?" She was born only a few weeks before land was sold on the West Van Nuys tract. So what do you think?

VICTOR HUGO

Mongram Avenue was named after the Monogram Home Builders. The company advertised that they built homes as "individualized as a personal monogram." Curiously, some of Mongram Avenue disappeared under today's Van Nuys Airport. As to Cagney Street... Yes, it was named after the screen actor James Cagney, who once owned a racehorse ranch in the Valley. Cagney acquired ownership of the ranch in 1953, which spans approximately 450 acres. In 1964, he sold the land for subdivision. And that was the year the street was named after him, James Francis Cagney, Jr. (shortened, of course).

Sesnon Boulevard honors three siblings who owned land in the Valley: Porter Sesnon, William T. Sesnon, and Barbara Sesnon. All three were essentially absentee landlords. They lived comfortably in their San Francisco mansions. When the last of their holdings, approximately 4,150 acres, was sold in 1962, it fetched $ 20 million. It's always nice to own a chunk of land...

JAMES CAGNEY

BEFORE THE SUBDIVISIONS

Granada Hills was named after the word for "pomegranate." The area was initially called Granada. The word Hills was added in 1942 to avoid confusion with a town in northern California. The land was acquired from, and you guessed it, George K. Porter. Besides farming beans and wheat, raising citrus fruits, and operating a dairy farm, there was an orchard called the Sunshine Ranch. J. H. Moshier (1855-1938) owned the land. He was a wealthy oilman from Oklahoma. The Suburban Estates Company later subdivided that land in the 1920s. That company was a holding company organized by the Edwards and Wildey Company. That company had subdivided Eagle Rock and portions of Glendale. With their financing and skills, they did so in Granada Hills.

WELCOME TO ANOTHER SUBDIVISION

THE 1950'S IN GRANADA HILLS, CA

Before moving on to a bit of trivia… Captain Butler and Mrs. J. L. Miller built the first house in Granada Hills, California. It was located at the corner of Kingsbury Street and White Oak Avenue. Before moving into the area, he was the Chief of Police in Los Angeles under Mayor Woodman (and another street sign).

It is time to go west. Chatsworth beckons, as do Encino and Reseda, other areas of the Valley.

A Personal Note

In 1968, a couple of modestly paid high school teachers got married. Before taking their final vows, they considered the future. You know, talking about kids amongst other things. Acting out of prudence and poverty, they decided to have three dependents. The first would be a house, after which they would add to the world's population. Later procreation proved easier than finding a home they could afford. For two years, they saved every penny they could. By 1970, they had $5,000 in the bank. Though bankrolled all efforts to purchase a home proved futile. Whether interest rates went up or down, almost everything was, it seemed, just out of their range.

Then they got lucky. They joined another couple for dinner. They happened to live in Northridge. To be more precise, they resided on Germain Street. While enjoying dinner, the house-hunting woes were discussed. This led to an unexpected response. "Hey, the house next door is up for sale. Check it out."

And so Bob and Jan Livingston did.

The house in question was not yet assigned to a real estate agent. That was supposed to happen the next day. An offer was quickly made and was accepted shortly thereafter. As to how we came up with the "additional" needed dough, well, that's a state secret. One onerous rumor should be dispelled. The two teachers didn't sell "A's" and a slick road to graduation. That is not to say, however, that the thought wasn't considered.

That's how we found our residence in Northridge. Fifty-plus years later, we're still here, fortunate enough to have okay health and a roof over our heads. Sometimes it's nice to live in a serendipitous world. It was for us.

CHAPTER 10 – CHATSWORTH

Several notable streets in Chatsworth include De Soto Avenue, Nordhoff Street, Shoup Avenue, and Winnetka Avenue. Let's talk about them before figuring out how Chatsworth got its name.

First, DeSoto Avenue was not named after the DeSoto automobile. You remember that car (if you're old enough). It was quite an automobile in its day, sleek, elegant, and in today's parlance, very cool.

The street sign honor goes to Hernando DeSoto. (1500-1542) His claim to fame rested on his exploits in leading the first European expedition into the southeastern portion of the United States (1539-1542). History records that he died on the banks of the Mississippi River. As good a place as any, I guess. Many years later, make that 1910, De Soto Avenue was laid out. At the time, the Suburban Homes Company owned the land after purchasing it from Isaac Van Nuys. The company set about transforming the San Fernando Valley from a predominantly agricultural area, dominated by wheat and cattle farming, into a residential and commercial hub.

As some have suggested, perhaps the men running the company saw themselves as latter-day conquistadors in suits rather than armor. Other streets, it seems, were also named after explorers, including Alvarado (now Woodley), Cabrillo (now Haskell), Cortez (now Fulton), and Diaz (now Coldwater). A coincidence? I don't think so.

HERNANDO DE SOTO

Nordhoff Street... I bet you, though, as did I, that the street was named after the celebrated writer of *Mutiny on the Bounty*. You were right. Charles Bernard Nordhoff (1887-1947) was the grandson of Charles Nordhoff. The grandson wrote the book. The street was named after him. So, what's the story?

The elder Charles Nordhoff (1830-1901) was a celebrated journalist who promoted California and convinced many to become transplants. For example, in 1872, he published a very favorable account of his visit to the state entitled *California: For Health, Pleasure, and Residence*. Some say that Collis P. Huntington hired him to do the job. Huntington was an executive with the Southern Pacific Railroad. Apparently, the book was a hit. In 1874, the Ventura County town of Nordhoff was named in his honor, even though the journalist never lived there. The name was short-lived. The citizens of the city changed it to Ojai because German names were exceedingly unpopular during World War I (Nordhoff had been born in Prussia). It wasn't until 1917 that the Nordhoff was honored with a street named after it in the Valley. Who would have guessed?

CHARLES NORDHOFF, CHARLES BERNARD NORHOFF

THE NOVEL

Shoup Avenue was named after Paul Shoup in 1917, when the City Council changed West Valley's Second Street to Shoup Avenue. Okay, that's the easy part. Shoup (1874-1946) gets his name on a street sign… But who was this guy you are asking about?

In 1891, Shoup got a job with the Southern Pacific Railroad after graduating from high school in San Bernardino. Beginning as a ticket seller, he rose in the ranks, becoming president of the railroad in time. Not a bad ride… It turns out that Shoup was also a short-story writer. In 1898, he combined his interests in literature and railroads by launching a unique publication under the auspices of the Southern Pacific Railroad. You know it as the *Sunset Magazine*. Shoup saw it as a good way to drum up business.

A good part of his railroad experience was in Northern California. In 1906, he was involved in laying tracks down the San Francisco Peninsula. In the process, he purchased 100 acres of land owned by Sarah Winchester to negotiate the rights to build a railroad station and a right-of-way. And yes, the seller was the owner of the mysterious Winchester Mystery House. You know… The house with way too many doors leading to nowhere… Anyway, the purchase of the land led to the development of a new town, Los Altos. In 1911, he moved to L.A. after his company bought the Pacific Electric Railroad from Henry Huntington. All of this led to his name being on a signpost.

PAUL SHOUP, THE MAGAZINE

THE WINCHESTER HOUSE

About Winnetka Avenue… A chicken farmer named Charles Weeks (1873-1964) did not name Winnetka Avenue after his hometown, Winnetka, Illinois. He was actually born in Swayzee, Indiana. He did have a poultry colony on Winnetka Avenue in 1922, but the street had been named five years earlier. That was before he came to LA. So, what happened? One plausible explanation refers to the letter "W." Did a civil engineer rename Walnut Avenue, Winnetka, in 1910 because both words began with the same letter? No one knows for sure. By the way, Winnetka is derived from a Native American term meaning "beautiful place."

THE CHICKEN FARMER MAKES GOOD

The suburb of Chatsworth is located in the northwest part of the San Fernando Valley, sheltered by the San Susana Mountains. The area was once home to the Cabielino Indians, who used a natural watering hole at the corner of Reseda and Parthenia Street. The suburb owes its name to the majestic Chatsworth House in England, near Chesterfield in Derbyshire. The name came from Samuel Bennington, who had a farm called Chatsworth Farm.

The area was first explored and colonized by the Spanish, beginning with the Portola Expedition on August 5, 1769. That was also the year that Spain established the San Fernando Mission. In 1874, the family of Eulogio F. de Celis sold their portions of Rancho Ex-Mission to three people: Charles Maclay, George K. Porter, and Benjamin F. Porter. Maclay's land was east of Sepulveda Boulevard, while the Porters got the land west of the street, including most of Chatsworth. George R. Crow first recorded the name Chatsworth Park in 1888. In 1915, the residents of Chatsworth voted to become part of L.A. with an emphasis on their Chatsworth name.

Over the years, the area was a fashionable location for Hollywood's biggest stars for ranches, raising horses. It was also where Lucille Ball and her husband had a five-acre ranch that they purchased for $16,000 in 1941. Besides celebrities, the area is also known for its geological formations, including the Garden of the Gods, Stoney Point Park, and the Iverson Movie Ranch. I wonder how Samuel Bennington felt about all that? Or for that matter, the Cabielino Indians?

OLD CHATSWORTH SIGN

CHATSWORTH, TOPANGA, AND DEVEONSHIRE, 1939

IVERSON MOVIE RANCH

It's time to leave Chatsworth… It's on to Sylmar and Pacoima.

CHAPTER 11 – SYLMAR

Sylmar has many streets honoring past American presidents. Polk Street has an unusual background. It all began in 1885. Some 20,000 acres of the Maclay Rancho subdivision were mapped out that year. In doing so, twenty streets were named for American presidents, beginning with George Washington and continuing to Grover Cleveland, who was then serving his first term. If you look for those street names, you won't find them today. So, what happened? Sixteen were renamed, leaving four for posterity. Tyler Street is named after the 10th president, John Tyler (1790-1862). Of course, Polk Street honors James K. Polk (1795-1849), the 11th president. Pierce Street is named after Franklin Pierce (1804-1869). He was the country's 14th president. Filmore Street is something of a challenge. The street was misspelled. The correct spelling is Fillmore, which honors the 13th president, Millard Fillmore (1800-1874).

Paxton Street has two possible origins. The first possibility honors Catherine Paxton Maclay (1824-1898). Her husband was Charles Maclay, the gentleman who founded the city of San Fernando. When the street was named in 1885 on the large Maclay Rancho tract, did the hubby honor his wife with a street name?

MRS. MACLAY, MR. MCLAY

The second possibility is this. The street is named after John Alexander Paxton (1819-1888). He was the director of the Los Angeles County Bank, along with other owners of the Maclay Rancho. Jonathan Sayre Slauson (1829-1905) and John E. Plater were the other owners. Each of them ended up on a street sign. Sayre Street is still around. Plater Street became Tuxford Street. And let's not forget Hugh L. Macneil (1850-1901), a co-owner of the Maclay Rancho tract.

Personal Note

"With a degree of questionable pride, I must point out that Macneil's middle name was Livingston. I like the sound of that. He was also a good-looking chap."

――――――――――

JONATHAN S. SLAUSON, HUGH L. MACNEIL

Nurmi Street is in Sylmar. It was named in 1925. The name is not Spanish. Nor is it English. Therefore, it must be Finnish. It was. Who was Nurmi, or Paavo Nurmi (1897-1973)? He was an international superstar in the 1920s. He held 22 world records in track (middle distance running) and earned nine Olympic gold medals. Now, as to the street sign... The assumption is that some civil engineer or possibly a developer was a track fan. Difficult to prove... Of course, it is equally challenging to disprove...

One more point... There's another street in Sylmar named after a world-class athlete. Trying to guess? It's Paddock Street. That street sign was named after Charley Paddock, an Olympic sprinter (1900-1943), in 1925. At the 1920 Olympics, he won two gold medals and one silver medal. In 1924, he tried to repeat the feat. It didn't work out. Harold Abrahams of England defeated him. Does that name sound familiar? Remember the film *Chariots of Fire?* That's the film in which England's finest beat the "world's fastest human." One last thing… Paddock went to USC. Go Trojans.

PAAVO NURMI, CHARLES PADDOCK

Roxford Street in Sylmar… What's the story here? A somewhat confusing one, I assure you. Roxford Street was laid out in 1885. At that time, it was named Jackson Street in honor of President Andrew Jackson (1767-1845). In 1915, the City of Los Angeles annexed the Valley. This led to a name change due to a postal conflict. There was already Jackson Street in L.A. Some believe Roxford is named after a rancher, but there is little evidence to support this claim. Another possibility deserves recognition, according to some. Did a civil engineer want a British-sounding name for Sylmar? After all, Beverly Hills had Roxbury and Rexford streets. Why not a little British luster for Sylmar? An urban myth inspires a long shot… At one time, the Roxford Knitting Company (located in Philadelphia) had a branch in L.A. Did this inspire some city official? Did he like fashionable underclothes? Could be.

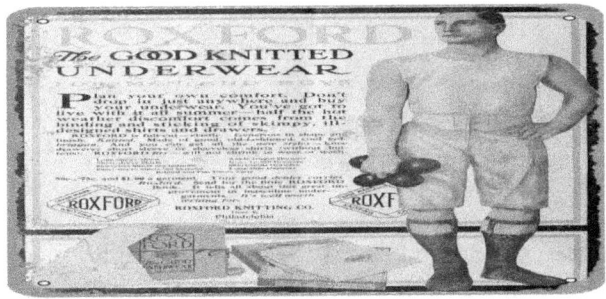

As to the Sylmar… The original name was Morningside, named after this lovely area in the foothills of the San Gabriel Mountains. That name didn't last. You can thank the humble olive for the name change. Historically, the area was characterized by a profusion of Sylvan olive orchards. In 1890, the Los Angeles Olive Growers Association got into the picture. It would grow and systematically harvest olives. By 1894, more than 1700 acres were planted with olive trees. By 1906, Sylmar housed the largest olive grove in the world. Well over 300 Japanese were hired and housed to serve the trees during the picking season. They lived in a village of tents. By 1927, the olive packing plant employed 500 workers during its busiest time of the year. Because of all this, Morningside had to redo. In 1893, the name was changed to Sylmar, a combination of two Latin words for "forest" and "sea." Together, the words suggested a "sea of trees," or, in this case, a sea of olive trees.

SYLMAR'S OLIVE INDUSTRY

CHAPTER 12 – PACOIMA

Some curious street names are also found in Pacoima, California, such as Jouett Street, Pinney Street, Montague Street, and Hoyt Street. Have you ever heard of them? Well, you're about to.

First, we begin with a misspelling. Jouett Street is named after Jewett Allin (1854-1936). Notice the spelling error. That seemed to be a common problem in newspapers in his day. In any event, the street was named in 1887. Jouett was the founding chief of Pacoima. He did so in conjunction with a team of investors. One was his father-in-law, Dr. Elbert Pinney (1826-1914). Another was Roscoe Hoyt 1819-1896). Together, they purchased 120 acres of the Maclay Rancho tract. Those acres became Pacoima.

JEWETT ALLIN, DR. ELBERT PINNEY, ROSCOE HOYT

Dr. Pinney has a fascinating background. He was a native of Connecticut. He received his medical degree in Ohio before setting up his practice in Illinois. All that was before he packed up his family and moved to Texas, where slavery was legal. There, he acquired five enslaved people, including two children. During the Civil War, he joined the Confederate Army as a surgeon. After the conflict, he moved to Duarte, CA, to raise oranges. Next came a career in real estate speculation. He also built a

Victorian hotel in Sierra Madre. That was in 1887. Today, it is a private residence called the Pinney House—quite a guy behind the street sign.

What's the story behind Montague Street? In 1915, the city of Los Angeles annexed a significant portion of the San Fernando Valley. This led to a duplication problem. What should be done about like-named streets in L.A. and the Valley? I'm sure you can guess. Lincoln Street became Osborne Street, and Grant Street (named for the General) was renamed Montague Street. But why that name? Lilian Anna Montague (1885-1956) was the wife of Henry Zenas Osborne, Jr. His brother, Sherrill Blasdel Osborne, was a big-time landowner. The street appears to have been named after Lilian. Notice all the connections.

THE PINNEY HOUSE, LILIAN ON THE LEFT

Hoyt Street honors George Washington Hoyt (1819-1896). He was an early investor in Pacoima and a captain during the Civil War, fighting for the Union. He came to California in 1875 to grow oranges near Los Angeles. Hoyt Street was named in 1887. Along with his wife, he spent his remaining days on Pinney Street.

A word about Pacoima... The name is tied to water, specifically a large stream that flows through the area. That's the easy part. The Ferandeno-Tongva and Tataviam tribal people first inhabited the area. The original name for the Native American village in the area was Pakoinga or Pakiynga. However, because the "ng" sound did not exist in Spanish, the good friars and soldiers mistook the sound for an "m" and recorded the name as Pacoima. Where was the Automobile Club to help the Spaniards?

Pacoima's earliest written record dates to 1769, when the Spanish explored the San Fernando Valley. That was the Portola expedition. Over time, and following the Mexican War, the area shifted from Mexican control to Yankee ownership, and the land rush was underway in the Valley. Land and a water supply whetted the appetites of speculators, and in time, the subdivision of land.

EARLY DOWNTOWN PACOIMA

AN EARLY ROAD IN PACOIMA

FELLOW TRAVELERS

CHAPTER 13 – SAN FERNANDO

Pico Street... Just another street in San Fernando... A short name with a complicated past... So, let's get to it.

Most people are familiar with the last governor of Alta California, at least when they hear his name. Pio Pico (1801-1894). But do you know his brother's name, Andres Pico (1810-1876)? So, which brother was the street named after? It appears to have been Andres Pico, but it could have been either brother.

Andres was a San Diego native. He moved to L.A. in 1844. He was a ranchero and an adjutant in the Mexican Army. In 1845, he secured a lease on land that the Mexican government had secularized. That is, land no longer controlled by the church. Now, who granted the land to him? That's right, his brother, Pio. During the Mexican-American War, he commanded Mexican forces in California. In 1847, he surrendered his troops to John C. Fremont (1813-1890) in the Treaty of Cahuenga. He served in the new California state legislature while controlling large portions of the San Fernando Valley. He sold his land holdings to his older brother to pay off large debts, who later resold the land to Isaac Lankershim (1818-1982). Indeed, that's a name you recognize. Some more trivia... Andres Pico Adobe was the oldest house in the Valley.

ANDRES PICO, JOHN C. FREMONT, ISAAC LANKERSHIM

ANDRES PICO ADOBE HOME

Henry William Griswold (1854-1887) ... Recognize the name? Probably not... Most people wouldn't. He was the son-in-law of Charles Maclay, a founder of San Fernando. Griswold married Mary Elizabeth Maclay (1860-1937) in 1887. He settled in the area in 1878. Griswold was hired as a station agent and telegraph operator at the local depot. Additionally, he was appointed justice of the peace in 1881. He also operated a general store and planted trees throughout San Fernando. Unfortunately, his life was short-lived. In 1887, he died of an undisclosed ailment. A street sign in his honor was dedicated sometime before his death. As you can see, you know how this street name came about.

HENRY WILLIAM GRISWOLD, MARY GRISWOLD

Mott Street was named after two brothers, Thomas Dillingham Mott (1829-1904) and Stephen Hathaway Mott (1828-1909). After arriving from upstate New York, they made their mark in real estate, industry, and government. Their first venture in California came during the "Gold Rush of 1849. They made their money running ferries across the San Joaquin River. That, of course, beats panning for gold nuggets. Once in L.A., Thomas convinced the Southern Pacific Railroad to extend tracks to the Southland. That was a considerable achievement. The brothers got involved in lumber companies and water and gas projects. They also owned a piece of real estate, which is now known as Bunker Hill. Though they have a street named after them, most of their presence was in Los Angeles.

THOMAS AND STEPHEN MOTT

Let's take a look at another street in San Fernando. Huntington Street is named after Collis Potter Huntington (1821-1900). The date for this was about 1887, when the street was first mentioned in the press. Huntington's fame came from his involvement in building the Central Pacific and Southern Pacific Railroads. He was one of the "Big Four" who did this, the others being Leland Stanford (think the university in Palo Alto), Mark Hopkins (recall the hotel in San Francisco), and Charles Crocker (banking in California). As with bringing water to the Valley, the construction of the transcontinental railway helped put the Golden State on the map, gold notwithstanding, in the Sacramento River.

COLLIS POTTER HUNTINGTON, THE GOLD RUSH

The City of San Fernando was founded in 1874. It was known as "The Mission City" because of Mission San Fernando Rey de España, established on September 8, 1797, by Fathers Fermin Lasuen and Francisco Dumetz. This you already knew. The mission was named after Saint Ferdinand. It was one of the twenty-one Spanish missions in Alta California. The graceful porticoes still stand today. The mission, of course, gave its namesake to the City of San Fernando and the San Fernando Valley. The city also takes its name after the valley in which it is located, "El Valle de San Fernando." The area around the Mission had abundant spring water for irrigation and drinking. There was also limestone in the nearby San Gabriel Mountains, which could be used to construct buildings.

The mission's founding dates back to the Spanish Portola expedition. The first Europeans camped at a watering hole on August 7, 1769, where the mission would later be constructed. Fray Juan Crespi was one of the Franciscan missionaries traveling with the explorers. He recorded that their camp was at "the foot of the mountains." He also noted the abundance of groundwater and the Mediterranean climate's graciousness.

THE MISSION

San Fernando was incorporated in 1911. And of importance... The City of Los Angeles never annexed it.

WORKING THE LAND

As already noted, the operative word in the Valley was the notion of subdivision, which would lead to sprawling housing developments. This happened in Northridge, Chatsworth, Granada Hills, and all the other enclaves defining the Valley. To a degree, the San Fernando Valley became a vast bedroom community offering a suburban lifestyle compared to living in densely packed urban areas. A little house… A backyard… Perhaps a pool… And a two-car garage. For many, it was a blessing not afforded in a tight little apartment where one had to pay for temporary occupancy every month. The gift of land, water, and subdivisions was the new American dream for many. But not for all…

At 62, Malvina Reynolds (1980-1978) wrote a sharp critique of the suburban lifestyle. That was in 1962. Her song was *Little Boxes*, just two minutes and eleven seconds of denouncing tract homes, bland aesthetics, and the death of creativity in suburbia. It was counterculture on steroids. She considered cookie-cutter homes the equivalent of cookie-cutter, standardized folks cloaked in uniformity and the loss of individualism. Her lyrics stung, but also stagnated. Then, a young folk singer recorded it in 1963, and it became a lively footnote to the 1960s. The singer was Pete Seeger. (1919-2014) A few of the verses follow.

Little boxes on the hillside
Little boxes made of ticky-tacky
Little boxes on the hillside
Little boxes all the same.

There's a pink one and a green one.
And a blue one and a yellow one
And they're all made out of tic-tac-toe
And they all look the same.

And the people in the houses
All went to the university
Where they were put in boxes
And they all came out the same.

Of course, those little "ticky-tacky" homes sell today for close to a million smackaroons. Many who fled to suburbia found Seeger's rendition lively and engaging as they sent their monthly check to Bank of America. PITI trumped ticky-tacky, a social satire notwithstanding.

TICKY-TACKY OR THE AMERICAN DREAM?

CONFORMITY HAS ITS VIRTUES

PETE SEEGER, MALVINA REYNOLDS

CHAPTER 14 – MISSION HILLS

Mission Hills, California, was once known as Hickson. It was renamed for he nearby Spanish Mission, which, as you will recall, was Mission San Fernando Rey de Espana 1784). How did that come about? Skip ahead in time, and the area was once called Dennis Park. That occurred when the area was subdivided in 1951. A few years later, the name was changed by a vote of the locals led by business interests. Read that, the Chamber of Commerce. In 1956, the deed was done. The old "Welcome to Dennis Park" sign was dismantled and repainted to read "Welcome to Mission Hills."

COLLECTING VOTES

If you live in the Valley, you've probably come across Kester Avenue, a busy street in Mission Hills. It was named after John Hambleton Kester, a tenant farmer (1828-1898). He lived in the San Fernando Valley for less than three years. So, you're asking, how did he get his name on a street sign? As a tenant farmer, he worked land owned by Isaac Lankershim and Isaac Van Nuys. It appears Kester met the two men while living in Napa County. After Pio Pico sold his property to Lankershim Kester, his family came to Los Angeles in 1876. The Kesters worked the land, growing wheat and barley on thousands of acres, mainly near present-day Van Nuys. The Ranch was called Kester Ranch. In 1910, the ranch land was subdivided, and Kester became a street sign.

A KESTER RANCH AUCTION

What does Aeleta mean? It is a girl's name, most probably of Old English origin. The distinct meaning of the word is "oath." That comes from the ancient practice of taking an oath or pledge, a solemn promise to fulfill an expectation or duty. Some say the origin of Arleta is found in the Spanish language, where the notion of a pledge is present.

Arleta Avenue was named in 1917, some four decades before a post office was established in the Arleta neighborhood. No one is quite sure who the street sign honors. One theory involves a successful real estate developer. His name was Thomas Benton Potter (1867-1916). He named five streets in different locations after his daughter, Natalia Arleta Potter (1893-1972), including Aaleta Avenue in Mission Hills. One such street was in San Francisco. Another was in Kansas City. Then there is Arleta Park in Half Moon Bay, and a Portland enclave now known as Mt. Scott-Arleta. That's one theory. Another view is that the developer combined the names of his daughters, Arlene and Anta, to create Arleta. Or, of course, did a nondescript civil engineer in L.A. know about Potter's developments and borrow the name, Arleta? So, take your choice.

NATALIA ARLETA POTTER, COMBINING NAMES

Wolfskill Street... Now there's an interesting name honoring someone in Arleta. William Wolfskill (1798-1866) owned extensive land holdings in Southern California. He was a successful winemaker credited with advancing the region's citrus industry, including the development of the Valencia orange. It would become the most popular orange juice in the country. The City of Valencia is named after the fruit. As to the wine business... At the time of his death, his efforts were yielding over 50,000 gallons of wine annually. He also made most of the table grapes enjoyed by Americans. In short, he was something. In time, his family members owned ranch land that eventually became Westwood. Go UCLA.

WILLIAM WOLFSKILL, ORCHARD SALE

Another street in Mission Hills is Halbrent Avenue. This street was named in 1939 by Hal B. Willis (1898-1986) and his wife, Louise Fazenda (1895-1962). They had one child, Hal Brent Wallis (1933-2006), who went by his middle name. That said, where does that leave us? Is the street named after the son? That appears to be the case.

Of course, most seniors would recognize Hal B. Wallis' name. While at Warner Brothers, he was involved in major films such as *Little Caesar*, *Jezebel*, *The Maltese Falcon*, and *Casablanca*. Through his own production company, he produced the original film adaptation of *True Grit*.

THE HAPPY COUPLE, CASABLANCA, THE BIRD

A Personal Note

In the 1970s, the Los Angeles School District (LAUSD) experimented in social planning. It implemented an unpopular program of "forced busing." Our daughter was in the second grade and attending Darby Elementary, a mere ten-minute walk from our home. Rachel was designated for a bus ride to Arleta Elementary School, a forty-minute ride, because it was necessary to pick up other children involved in the program. As parents, we were faced with a difficult choice. Abide by the Board's mandate, or consider placing our child in a private school or one of the burgeoning homeschool programs. After much soul searching, we participated in the busing scheme, even as many of our friends engaged in what would later be called "white flight."

Rachel attended Arleta Elementary for one year. She was the only Anglo girl in the class of almost exclusively Hispanic children. She was also far ahead of most kids in reading, which led her to be an assistant to the teacher. She helped her peers with their reading. Academically, Rachel didn't make significant progress that school year. Socially, she did. She acquired some Spanish and was invited to birthday parties, usually the only Anglo girl. After one year, we applied for and were accepted into a highly gifted elementary school, San Jose Street Gifted Elementary, in Mission Hills. She was still being bused, but now in a more demanding academic environment.

Sometimes, being a caring parent and a good citizen can be challenging. Participating in a magnet program meant later entry into Portola Middle School's highly gifted program and then successful work at Grandaa Hills High School, our home school.

CHAPTER 15 – NORTH HILLS

North Hills was once called Mission Acres and later Sepulveda. That was before becoming North Hills in 1991. That year, the residents of the western half of Sepulveda, west of the San Diego Freeway, voted to secede from the eastern section to form a new community. Not to be outdone, the City of Los Angeles changed the name of the remaining portion of Sepulveda to North Hills. But that wasn't the end of it. The city created a new "sub-neighborhood" of North Hills West, which began west of the 405. The eastern section became North Hills East. Some say all the changes masked an attempt by residents to protect, if not increase, the value of their properties. Take on a more prosperous-sounding name. Dissociate your area from Sylmar, Sepulveda, Mission Hills, and San Fernando. Link yourself, as far as possible, to the more prosperous area of Northridge. That seemed to be the impulse behind the name changes.

Schoenborn Street in North Hills was named after a mortgage lender, Lawrence "Harry" Schoenborn (1891-1929). He named the street after himself. That was in 1926. He owned a tract of land between Topanga Canyon Boulevard and Canoga Avenue. Nice piece of real estate… By all accounts, he was an accomplished man, financially prosperous, and highly regarded in the real estate industry. This, of course, leads to a troubling question. Why did he commit suicide on April 17, 1929? He parked in the garage of a building he owned in Los Angeles, closed the garage door, and died of carbon monoxide poisoning. A sad story… Time to move on to Gothic Avenue.

"HARRY"

There is no frightening story behind this street name, at least as far as I know. No sinister history lurks in the shadows of North Hills. Still, the name is gloomy. According to a city ordinance, it all occurred in December 1916. Why was this? After the City of Los Angeles annexed the Valley, a problem arose. Some Valley streets were duplicates of street names in Los Angeles proper. That, as you know, necessitated a change. Originally, Gothic Street was Santa Barbara Place. Now that sounds nice. Lots of sun and balmy weather… But, as you've already guessed, there was already a Santa Barbara Avenue in L.A. An unknown civil servant chose the name Gothic, it is assumed, from a list of potential names. Who knows? Maybe the choice was made because the guy liked Halloween.

The origin of the word goes back to an extinct Germanic language. The 4th-6th centuries A.D. Gothic also relates to a style of architecture in later centuries characterized by pointed arches, rib vaults, and flying buttresses, all tied together with large windows. Hard to find a house like that in North Hills…

A last word… The adjective gothic describes something characterized by mystery, horror, and gloom, especially in literature: Hello, Edgar Allan Poe and the memorable opening lines of *The Raven*.

Once upon a midnight dreary, while I pondered, weak and weary,

Over many a quaint and curious volume of forgotten lore,
While I nodded, nearly napping, suddenly there came a tapping,
As of some one gently rapping, rapping at my chamber door."
"Tis some visitor," I muttered, "taping at my chamber door---
Only this and nothing more."

Parthenia Street crosses through many locations in the Valley, including Chatsworth, North Hills, Northridge, and Panorama City. Nothing exceptional about the naming of this street, as you will see... Chappel Quillian "C.Q." Stanton was a developer (1852-1926). He named the street in honor of his daughter, Parthenia Hale Stanton (1913-1976). She was a graduate of what is now called Harvard-Westlake School. She also attended UCLA. After marrying Francis Sellers McComb, she named a daughter Parthenia Peyton McComb. That kept the name in the family. Some more trivia... Cedros Avenue was once called Hale Avenue. That was Parthenia's middle name, as you will recall.

Parthenia, by the way, is feminine and means "maiden," "virgin," or "chaste." It is derived from the Ancient Greek word meaning "virgo." It was an exceptional choice for babies born in late August or September. Perhaps Parthenia's father knew all this. Who knows for sure?

PARTHENIA, WILLIAM (TOP ROW, SECOND FROM LEFT)

Petit Avenue (see above) was named after William Justin Petit (1876-1948), a Valley pioneer who was honored in 1916. Petit grew up in Oxnard, attended USC, and later ran a very successful sugar beet farm. His son, Stanley Norris Petit (1904-2000), was one of the first inhabitants of the Valley to own an airplane. He was also the first to land a plane at Van Nuys Airport in 1928.

Woodley Avenue was initially called Alvarado Avenue. The name was changed once the City of Los Angeles annexed the San Fernando Valley. Duplication was the rascal here. L.A. already had an Alvarado Street. That being the case, a street name was needed. Alvarado Avenue became Woodley Avenue. It was named after Frank Erwin Woodley (1865-1934). Once in California, he entered the real estate business and ventured into citrus growing, water companies, and mines. He also had a political bug. He was elected to the California legislature in 1912. Later, he ran for the LA City Council and lost. After that, he was appointed to the Country Board of Supervisors.

FRANK E. WOODLEY, STREET SIGN

If you live on Lassen Street, that road honors a man who was shot to death while prospecting for silver near Nevada's Black Rock Desert. His killer was never discovered. So what's the story on this guy? Peter Lassen was a Danish immigrant (1800-1859) with several trades. He was a blacksmith, rancher, and explorer in California. He hit it big in the Mexican territory. Don Pedro Lassen was deeded over 22,000 acres comprising the Rancho Bosquejo. This was near present-day Susanville, in Lassen County, which was formed in 1864. I'm sure you surmised that Lassen National Park was our Mr. Lassen.

THE MAN AND THE PARK

CHAPTER 16 – PANORAMA CITY

A Personal Note

In 1962, I left San Francisco for greener hills in the Southland. That is to say, I had a teaching job in Los Angeles. The Los Angeles School District assigned me to Patrick Henry Junior High in the Valley. I got my first apartment in Panorama City with almost no knowledge of the area. My new principal had suggested the area as a nice place to be. He said it had inexpensive rental units, lovely shops, and a pleasant climate. I followed his advice. It was a nice area. Of course, I never considered for a moment how the enclave got its name. I just moved into my small apartment and began my life as a public school teacher. I guess that's the way it is for most people. Get a job, find a place to live, or do this in reverse...

Panorama City was the San Fernando Valley's first planned community. The credit for this honor goes to a residential developer, one Fritz B. Burns (1899-1979), and an industrialist, Henry J. Kaiser (1882-1967). Both men realized that a post-war demand for housing might work to their economic benefit. World War II vets were returning home and, spurred by the G.I. Bill, could attend college and purchase a home with a low-down payment and federal backing. In 1945, Burns and Kaiser formed Kaiser Community Homes. They were primed for the housing boom that fueled the Valley's population boom. Panorama City found a home in an area originally part of one of the largest dairy and sheep ranches in Southern California. In fact, Panorama City was named after the Panorama Dairy and Sheep Ranch.

HENRY J. KAISER, FRITZ B. BURNS

Interestingly, the homes built represented a new technology perfected during the war by Kaiser—"pre-milled and shop-fabricated"—by Kaiser's shipbuilders in a factory near present-day LAX. Everything for the house was delivered on site and assembled in a few weeks. In time, the popularity of the homes brought upwards of 5,000 people to view the model homes. If you made a purchase, the price was only $10,000. Talk about a good deal...

A TYPICAL KAISER BUILT HOME

WELCOME TO PANORAMA CITY

Lots of streets run through Panorama City. Let's begin with Mammoth Avenue. The name starts with three popular hot springs and a trio of names. Three streets were named on the track of land in 1923: Mammoth, Matilija, and Murietta. Keep that in mind... Murietta was initially spelled "Murrieta" and was tied to Murrieta Hot Springs in Riverside County. Then there was Matilija, which shares a name with the town of Ojai, and the Matilija Hot Springs are located there. Mammoth is related to the Mammoth Hot Springs located in Yellowstone National Park. It looks like the developers were into hot springs. Could be. Of course, some might argue that Murietta was named after Juan Murrieta (1844 - 1936). He was a Spaniard who owned a ranch in the area.

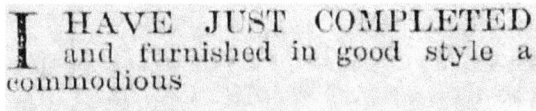

HAVE JUST COMPLETED and furnished in good style a commodious

HOTEL BUILDING

AT THE

HOT SPRINGS

IN THE

MATILIJA CANYON,

16 miles north of

SAN BUENAVENTURA

(Ventura County, Cal.),

OJAI HOT SPRINGS JUAN MURRIETA

Vesper Avenue honors Frank Horn Vesper (1858-1843). He established the Bank of Glendale. Years later, the bank was acquired by the Los Angeles Trust and Savings Bank. He also owned at least one track of land on which Vesper Street was laid out in 1915. As an aside… The term vesper refers to an evening prayer, service, or hymn. The word has other possibilities. In Greek, Vesper is the evening star that appears in the sky at sunset. That's in the western sky. That star is usually Venus. In Latin, the word translates literally to "evening star." And one more point… Vesper can also refer to lighting lamps during evening prayer services or the Eucharist in the evening.

113

Did Moses Sherman (1853-1932) name Hazeltine Avenue after one of his daughters? It appears so. After all, he had already named Sherman Oaks and Sherman Way to honor his family. As to the word's origin… It is an English surname that means "someone who lives near hazel trees." It is a name linked to nature and the landscape. However, the name can also refer to an ancient manor in Sussex near Dallington. Having our British cousins tied to our street names is always lovely.

HAZELTINE (SECOND FROM LEFT

A Personal Note

For those who know the Valley, the following photograph should bring back memories.

THE ORIGINAL KAISER HOSPITAL

The iconic building with its twin towers has vivid memories for our family. It was there that our two children were born. There, earaches in the night called for a hurried drive to urgent care. It was there that the doctors removed my gall bladder and, over the years, did a few other things. It was at the renovated Kaiser structure that Jan discovered that a blemish on the skin was cancer. It was also there that the cancer was stopped in its tracks. Lots of memories...

Recall that we bought a home on Germain Street in 1970. The owner was a doctor who worked at Kaiser. In negotiating a final price, I pointed out that we were essentially broke with only $500 in the bank and the first teacher strike on the immediate horizon. This led to a few requests on our part. Would the doctor leave the somewhat worn kitchen table and chairs? Would he leave the large pink refrigerator? And finally, would he leave the well-used washer and dryer? He did so, partially because he had just bought a new house and furnished it with the "latest."

About fifteen years later, I almost choked on a tiny piece of a pear. I was at Van Nuys High School at the time. After a fellow teacher applied the Heimlich procedure and popped out the pesky pear, I was sent to Kaiser. The medical guys said I had a problem swallowing. My esophagus can narrow when I'm stressed. The doctors wanted me to swallow a rubber bulb and a few feet of tubing. The idea was this: they would pump up the bulb, expand in my esophagus, and make it easier for me to swallow. All of this would be done while awake. Having almost choked on that nasty pear, I asked if there was another way to handle this. "Yes," they said, "we can put you under." "If you insist," I replied.

A week later, I went into the hospital for the procedure… Into the operating room came the doctor whose home I had purchased years earlier. Before they knocked me out, I said, "Doc, if I didn't pay enough, I'll write another check." As only a physician can tell, he smiled and said, "Turn on your side."

CHAPTER 17– WINNETKA

The history of Winnetka began in 1920 when the Los Angeles Chamber of Commerce sent out a request to Charles Weeks (1873-1964). He was invited to the San Fernando Valley to establish a series of one-acre egg farms. That's right… Egg farms… Weeks had gained notoriety in East Palo Alto, Northern California, for successfully developing egg farms. To that end, he established the Weeks Poultry Colony. To a degree, it was a utopian enterprise. Families with an entrepreneurial bent and who wanted to be financially independent were those Weeks sought for the 600 acres he owned and subdivided. He sold off one-acre lots to those inclined to be in the egg business. This original community was called Runnymede. The name would be changed to Owensmouth and later to present-day Winnetka.

In time, Weeks renamed the colony Winnetka after a farm he once owned in Winnetka, Illinois. That's one possibility. That was in 1922. Another view suggests that a civil engineer was enthralled with the "W's" in Weeks and Winnetka. And that's how the street got its name. Just a possibility…In any event, Weeks essentially put the colony on the map. Winnetka is a Native American word meaning "beautiful land." To the folks who live in the area today, that is an appropriate name, assuming they know about it.

Charles Weeks

Ingomar Street in Winnetka is not named after an explorer, a real estate developer, a railroad tycoon, or a financial baron. No, it's named after a stage play entitled *Ingomar, the Barbarian.* Yes, you read the words correctly. The play premiered in Austria in 1842 as *Der Sohn der Widnis*: "The Son of the Wilderness." An Austrian aristocrat wrote that lively play. He did so under the pen name, "Friedrich Halm." An English translation was made in 1851 and became an instant hit on both sides of the Atlantic. As late as 1933, the play was still being staged in the United States. Emory and Harriet Brace, named a decade earlier, were the landowners of considerable influence on Ingomar Street. One assumes they were big fans of the stage production and its most famous line:

Two souls with but a single thought, two hearts that beat as one...

In 1908, W. D. Griffith produced a film based on the stage play. Now that's cool.

THE FILM ADAPTATION

Londelius Street is named after Harry M. Londelius, Jr. (1918-1999). He landed in Los Angeles after a stint in the Navy during World War II. Here, he became an architect, designing numerous apartment buildings. Londelius was acquainted with lots of developers. It is assumed that one of them named a street in his honor. Another possibility concerns Frank and Helen Brick. They owned the 1954 track on which the street existed and was called. Did Londelius work for them? Did they name the street after him? Uncertainty rules here.

A curious fact… Londelius designed a house on Dilling Street. The Brady Bunch television series used that house as the Brady home. It was located in Studio City. The exact address: 11222 Dilling Street. Ah, for the age of television innocence.

LONDELIUS IS SECOND FROM THE LEFT (1965)

THE BRADY BUNCH AND THE DILLING STREET HOME

CHAPTER 18 – WOODLAND HILLS

Let's get right at it. In 1922, Victor Girard Kleinberger (1880-1954) bought 2,886 acres from a group headed by Harry Chandler of *L.A. Times* fame. In that year, he founded the town of Girard. He hoped to attract residents and businesses by developing a city, which we might today call an infrastructure. He achieved this through advertising and by planting 120,000 trees, including 300 pepper trees, as well as fir, pine, sycamore, and eucalyptus trees. The pepper trees in particular formed a canopy over Canoga Avenue between Ventura Boulevard and Saltillo Street. He did all this to attract residents.

Kleinberger was trying to create "small hillside country estates." Small was he operating word. Most valley subdivision lots at the time were about 80 acres. This visionary land developer was pushing against the grain. He carved out 6,828 lots from 2,886 acres. And, now lacking in modesty, he named the new community after himself. Now he just had to get people to see their potential home. He did so in a way that would have delighted Madison Avenue.

Those interested could purchase an undeveloped parcel for as little as $500. For $1,525, you can buy a four-room house designed in the Moorish style. The most common purchase was a small home selling for $998.00. Those were really the "good old days."

THE TOWN OF GIRARD IN 1924

THE BUILDER AND HIS ADS

By 1939, the area had small businesses but remained primarily agricultural. During the war years, Girard was incorporated into the City of Los Angeles. In 1945, it got a new name: Woodland Hills. A quick point… Because of his German-sounding name, he was required to change it during World War II. The last name was dropped. The middle name replaced it: Girard.

There are many interesting street names in Woodland Hills, California. One is Queen Florence Lane, and the other is Queen Victoria Road. One debunked view claimed Michael Curtiz named the two streets. He was the Hollywood director of *Casablanca* fame. True, he once lived in Girard on an estate built for him in 1934. But here's the problem. He didn't have any daughters named Florence and Victoria. There was, however, a real estate speculator who did. His name was Graham Watson Dible (1906-1971). He had two daughters: Florence Dible and Elizabeth Victoria Dible. Dible subdivided Curtiz's property and named the two streets in 1957. It appears, therefore, that the land speculator named the two streets for his kids.

FLORENCE AND VICTORIA

Some streets in Woodland Hills are easy to figure out. One such street is Owensmouth Avenue. "Owens" refers to the Owens River, which is located 200 miles north of the San Fernando Valley. "Mouth" refers to the mouth of the river where water enters the San Fernando Valley. The street name was coined in 1911 to celebrate the arrival of water through the Los Angeles Aqueduct project. Some believe Harrison Gray Otis *(L.A. Times)* came up with the name. William Mulholland didn't name the street. That's for sure. And by the way… Owensmouth was also the name of another community in the Valley. Apparently, the residents hated the name and jettisoned it in 1931. They renamed their town Canoga Park.

Vicente de la Ossa (1808-1861) … Ever hear of him? After arriving in Los Angeles in 1832, he became, in time, a prominent Angeleno. He owned a tavern and held various public offices. He owned considerable land, beginning with Rancho Providencia (today's Burbank). In 1849, he sold that property to buy Rancho Los Encinos. His adobe home still stands in Los Encinos State Historic Park. You can visit it.

As an aside… In Spanish, adobe refers to a mudbrick or some earthen construction. Adobe structures are highly durable. Adobe homes are cool in the summer and warm in the winter. However, unless they are reinforced, they are highly susceptible to earthquakes.

VICENTE de la OSSA, THE ADOBE

Del Valle Street proved both amusing and confusing. See what you think. Our old friend Victor Girard was inspired by the Valley's Spanish and Mexican legacy. That said, there is a strong case to be made that he named Del Valle Street after Ygnacio de Valle (1808-1880). So who was this person? To understand him, we must discuss Del Valle Drive. That street is in the Carthay Circle area. Carthay, what? That's right—two streets named after the same guy.

Carthay Circle is in Los Angeles, which some refer to as "Mid-City," or Central L.A. Wilshire Boulevard bounds the neighborhood to the north, Olympic Boulevard to the south, Fairfax Avenue to the east, and Schumacher Drive to the west. The city of Beverly Hills is located on the west side and has all that? The area was initially named Cathay Center. It was one of the first planned communities in Los Angeles.

Del Valle was a Mexican soldier who came to California in 1825. Over time, he was granted enormous tracts of land, beginning with half of Rancho El Tejon in present-day Kern County. He also inherited Rancho Camulos near Piru. That spot on the map, some say, inspired the setting for Helen Hunt Jackson's 1884 hit novel, *Ramona*. Del Valle was, as it turns out, the last Mexican alcalde (magistrate or mayor) in Los Angeles before California statehood.

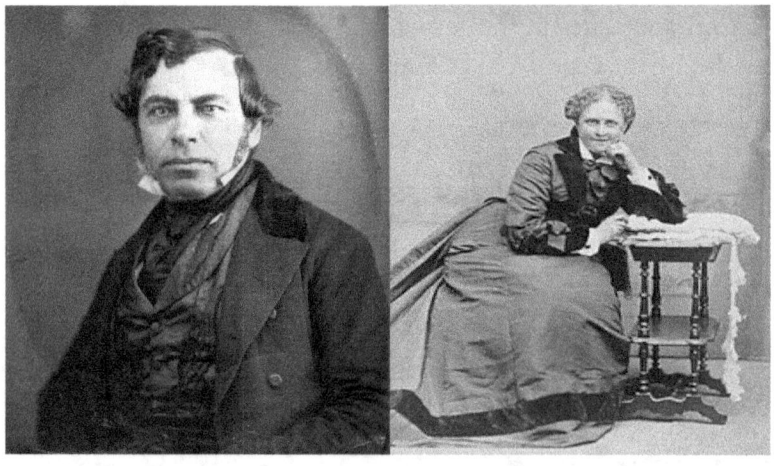

YGNACIO de VALLE, HENEN HUNT JACKSON

Having said all this, what is the connection between the two streets named after the same guy?

Del Valle had a son. His name was Reginaldo Francisco "R.F." de Valle (1854-1938). He was a member of the California legislature. He was also a close friend of J. Harvey McCarthy. Okay, so what, you're asking? He was the developer of Carthay Circle. He asked "R.F." and two other men to name the streets in the community. The request came with one injunction. The roads had to be named after California pioneers. You can see where this is going. The son named a street after his father.

CHAPTER 19 – SNOW IN THE VALLEY

Check out the photograph below.

That little house has a special history. First, it's located on Independencia Street in Woodland Hills. The street name is derived from a Spanish word that translates to "independence" in English. That might allude to Mexico overthrowing Madrid's control in the New World, or the California Bear Flag Rebellion against Mexico City, if one is so inclined to make that connection.

The bungalow-style house features three bedrooms, all of which are adequate but modest in size. The living room is equipped with a cozy fireplace and large windows that let in plenty of sunlight. Though it is difficult to see, there is a rather large backyard that extends up a hill and is ripe for terracing. The house does have two quirks. The front door is on the side of the house. The garage is detached.

In 1948, a World War II veteran took advantage of the G.I. Bill and put down $500 on the lot. He didn't have another $500 to purchase the adjacent lot. That vet was John Merrit Lobenstein. He was my wife's father. That's right, my Jan. With architectural plans drawn up by his brother, Wally, John and Lila (his wife) constructed their own home. You got that right. They didn't hire a private company to build the house.

John was a fireman with the LAFD and a skilled roofer, a trade he learned before the war. With the help of other firefighters, he first built the detached garage. As it turned out, the firemen all had construction skills, which they used to supplement their income. They all pitched in. As to their pay (if any), I am unsure. I do know they drank a considerable amount of 101 beer, an ancient brand. The beer cans were not thrown away. They were collected and then used to make a fence. Imagine the usual fence construction: 4x4s and 2.. That was a fence to drink to.

A word about Jan's mother... She worked alongside the men in building the latter-day adobe. She could swing a hammer with the best of the men and was no slouch at sewing a 4 X4. Always good to have a gal like that when you're building your own home. Of course, it didn't hurt that she was a Girl Scout Troop leader who certainly earned a merit badge for the way she pitched in with the men.

The family lived in the garage for over a year as the main house was built. Living in the garage required specific, unusual adjustments. The privacy issue was addressed by hanging blankets on rope lines. Without a restroom, a commode was used. There was no GE refrigerator. Portable ice chests were needed. There was no O'Keefe and Merritt stove. Instead, the family of four used an old-fashioned potbelly stove for cooking and heating. To put it that way, it was like living in a makeshift tent or an RV without pneumatic tires.

The house was still being built in January 1949 when the unexpected occurred. The temperature fell below freezing… Storm clouds appeared in the sky. And then it happened. Woodland Hills experienced a significant snowstorm that closed roads and schools. The storm began on a Monday and lasted several days. How bad was the snow? It was so deep that it made the intersection of Ventura and Topanga Canyon Boulevards impassable. As expected, cars skidded, and chains were advised. At least a foot of snow fell from the heavens. Can you beat that? Yes, all that happened in sunny and sometimes inordinately hot Woodland Hills. It was a belated Bing Crosby "White Christmas."

CAN YOU BELIEVE IT?

THIS IS SUNNY CALIFORNIA

That's the story of a little house in Woodland Hills.

A PERSONAL NOTE - Independencia was unpaved. The closest post office to Jan's home was Max's Saddle Shop. And once the house was built, a phone connection was established, along with those of seven other families. So, did you know when the ring was for you? Understand that all eight families were on the same line. The Lobenstein household listened for four rings. Less than that, or more, meant someone else was receiving a call. Somehow, the system worked. Ah, for the good old days.

CHAPTER 20 – CANOGA PARK

It all began in 1893. In that year, the Southern Pacific Railroad, then known as the Burbank-Chatsworth line, reached the small Canoga railroad station. From that point on, the community underwent several name changes. We'll get to those, but first, a question. What does Canoga mean?

Canoga is a Cayuga Iroquois word meaning "sweet water." Since the railroad station was near an old well, it seems plausible that someone with the railroad translated the Iroquois word as "watering hole." That worked with steam engines that need, of course, lots of water. In time, the Canoga community grew up around that railroad stop.

THE TRAIN STATION

The name stayed until 1911. In that year, Harrison Gray Otis got into the picture. Recall he was the publisher of the *Los Angeles Times*. That gave him lots of juice. He used it to rename the community Owensmouth, apparently to honor the forthcoming aqueduct that carried water from the Owens River. This was one year after Canoga Avenue was named. A considerable number of folks didn't like Otis' contribution to the map. Led by Mary "Mollie" Orcutt (1872-1973), they sought a name change. That name would be Canoga Park.

Mary's husband was William Warren Orcutt (1869-1942). He was an early developer of petroleum deposits in the Los Angeles area. He was also a petroleum geologist for the Unocal/Union Oil Company. While seeking black gold, he sauntered into the City's past. It's a very distant past. He discovered fossils in the La Brea Tar Pits, not too far from USC's campus. That was in 1901. The bones are related to the last Ice Age. What was unearthed? The Pleistocene coyote, that's what. It was named "cannis orcutti" in his honor. One could argue that beats a street name.

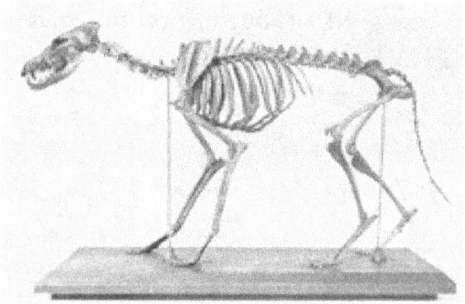

ORCUTT'S FIND

In addition to all this… At one time, William Orcutt owned over 4,000 acres of land in what is now the Granada Hills and Chatsworth areas. He used the land to raise cattle. In 1906, the Southern Pacific Railroad purchased much of his property for its right-of-way through the San Fernando Valley. Over time, the family heirs sold their holdings for subdivision.

However, the family was honored with a street name for "William Warren." This was Orcutt Drive in Montebello, California. What's the story here? Wasn't he a Valley man? Well, yes, he was. But he also had business dealings in Montebello. A street was named after him in 1960. He had helped to subdivide the area back in 1912. Influential in the Valley and honored elsewhere.

MARY (ON LEFT), WILLIAM

Mary Orcott's naming of Canoga Park led to, though it is hard to believe, a later mini-civil war in the western end of the San Fernando Valley. Want to know more? Of course you do. Recall that the area was initially called Owensmouth back in 1912 before being renamed Canoga Park in 1931. In 1987, residents, under the leadership of Joel Schiffman, began a petition campaign to secede in a three-square-mile area from Canoga Park. Advocates of the change had an economic argument. The name change would result in an immediate 5% increase in the value of homes in the new town, which would be called West Hills. The Canoga Park Chamber of Commerce strongly opposed the movement for separation. A bitter struggle ensued in the streets and before the L.A. City Council. Ultimately, a new area was carved out of Canoga Park. Thus was born West Hills.

Getting back to Canoga Park before the naming strife… Lots of streets run through Canoga Park, some of which we've already discussed: De Soto Avenue, Ingomer Street, Owensmouth Avenue, and Shoup Avenue. No need for a repeat. That being the case, let's look at a few streets in West Hills and what was once Canoga Park.

Some streets have amusing names. Take, for example, Bobbyboyar Avenue and Dannyboyar Avenue. You read it right. Both roads were named in 1856 on a subdivision owned by two brothers, Louis Boyar (1896-1976) and Mark Boyar (1901-1975). The brothers had purchased the land (875 acres of the old Platt Ranch) for $6.12 million. In developing the area, they had some fun with names. To begin with, there are no Roberts or Daniels in the Boyar family. Therefore, they didn't name the streets after any family member. "Bobby Boy" appears to be nothing more than a pun for a common nickname for Danny. Is this what motivated the Irish brothers? Perhaps… Or had they taken a liking to "a famous Irish Band or possibly a song written in 1910 by an English lawyer and lyricist. His name was Frederic Wealtherly (1848-1929). The song was, of course *Danny Boy*. The melody and lyrics still haunt us to this day.

Oh, Danny boy, the pipes are calling
From Glen O' Glen, and down the mountainside.
The summer's gone, and all the roses falling,
It's you, it's you who must go, and I must bide.
But come ye back when summer's in the meadow,
Or when he valley's hushed and while with snow,
I'll be here in sunshine or in shadow,
Oh, Danny boy, Oh Danny boy, I love you so!
But when ye come, and all the flowers are dying,
If I am dead, as dead I well may be,
Ye'll come and find the place where I am lying,
And kneel and say an Ave there for me.
And I shall hear, through soft you tread above me,
And all my grave will warmer, sweeter be,
For you will bend and tell me that you love me,
And I shall sleep in peace until you come to me!

FREDRIC WEATHERLY'S MUSIC

It's always nice to have a street in your community named after a famous actor. Does the name Frantisek Lederer ring a bell? Probably not… Lederer Avenue in West Hills was named after Francis Lederer (1899-2000) in 1956. He found his way to Hollywood in 1933 after a successful acting career in Europe, most notably in Germany following World War I. His breakthrough was when he teamed with Louise Brooks (1906-1985) in the classic silent film, *Pandora's Box* (1929). It was a smash at the box office and an instant hit internationally.

In the Hollywood studio world, he earned a substantial income, most of which he invested in real estate. In 1934, he bought a ranch in the West Hills area. His ranch was approximately 300 acres. Lederer Avenue is near where the old ranch once existed. News clippings indicate that he was a rather popular local figure, to the extent that he was appointed Honorary Mayor of Canoga Park in 1960.

A little trivia… *Pandora's Box* (1929) was about Lu Lu, a very seductive young woman with, to put it mildly, an uninhibited nature. Therein lies the plot line. She brings ruin to herself and others, particularly those who loved her. A cavorting lifestyle was destined to include murder, blackmail, a contentious trial, and a sad ending in squalor. Sounds like a perfect sit-com for today's audience.

THE ACTOR, THE ACTRESS, LU LU

A word to the wise… Be especially alert if you meet a "Lu Lu " on some dark evening. Be polite and persistent. You're safer at Lu Lu's Restaurant at Balboa and Roscoe. That's particularly true of older gents. Got the picture?

Platt Avenue is another well-known street in West Hills. The street sign honors George Edward Platt (1862-1936). Originally from Waterbury, Connecticut, he arrived in Los Angeles in 1882. In time, he bought land and established a dairy in East L.A. He was credited as the first dairyman to sell milk in glass bottles. If that's the case, it was only in California. Why is that? The first glass bottle was patented in 1878. It was called the Lester Milk Jar. Milk was sold in bottles for the first time a year later. That honor seems to go to Alex Campbell, a milk dealer from Brooklyn. He was using a glass bottle perfected by George Henry Lester. Eight decades later, the bottle went the way of all flesh. The culprit was the introduction of blown-molded plastic bottles (1960s). In with the new... Out with the old...

THE LOWLY MILK BOTTLE

Prospering in this endeavor, he purchased and leased thousands of acres in the Valley. In 1912, he hit it big. Platt purchased 1,109 acres encompassing the Rancho El Escorpion. He named a main road in the area Platt Road (now Platt Avenue).

––––––––––––––

A Personal Note

A confession, but one that has nothing to do with the Valley... I grew up in San Francisco's Richmond District, a pleasant area near the Presidio. One of my fondest childhood memories concerns Jerry. This guy drove a worlds Borden milk truck up and down our block each day. The truck was not refrigerated, at least not as we do today. The car was packed with large blocks of ice that kept the milk, cottage cheese, and ice cream cold. On a rare occasion during the summer when the temperature climbed into the high 80s, Jerry would crack a large block of ice and hand out chunks to all the kids. Crunching on the ice was so cool.

Here's an interesting question… How did the housewives tell Jerry what they needed, especially if they weren't home? Try to imagine your hand as heavy as colored paper. Your thumb stands for milk, and your little finger for cream. The cottage cheese is for the cottage cheese. Each finger, so to speak, represented a dairy product. Now place your hand in an empty milk container, fingers outstretched. Jerry noted which fingers were out and left the desired ones. If no fingers, no order… Straightforward… After a while, he had a pretty good idea of what each family wanted. You don't have service like that today.

THE BORDEN DAIRY

Some of you are old enough to remember the Helms Bakery truck rolling down the street and people pouring out of their homes to purchase cake, donuts, pies, all those tempting and sinful confections loaded with joyous sugar. That was in addition to bread and buns. In 1930, Paul Helms started the Helms Bakery with 32 employees and 11 trucks (called coaches). This was at the corner of Venice and Washington in Los Angeles. He was a former New Yorker who moved his family to the Golden State. In 1932, his company became the "Official Baker" of the Olympic Games held in Los Angeles. The Helm's motto was "Daily at Your Door." Each truck had an assigned neighborhood. As he drove through the area, the driver would sound a whistle, alerting all that good things could be had. In some cases, a large "H" was placed in a window to get the driver's attention. The business lasted until the 1970s, as did Elise the Cow.

PAUL HELMS

THE GOOD OLD DAYS

There is one street in Canoga Park/West Hills that claims our attention. In fact, that street begins where the I-118 (Ronald Reagan Freeway) enters the Valley from the west and continues southward through the Valley, across and over the Santa Monica Mountains all the way to the Pacific

137

Coast Highway. There, the Topanga Canyon Boulevard reaches a state beach honoring the road (Topanga State Beach near Pacific Palisades). The boulevard is also known as State Route 27. It is a major commuter route for those traveling between the San Fernando Valley and Santa Monica. Constructing this road was no easy task, as the following photos indicate.

TOUGH TERRAIN

TWISTING AND TURNING

WHERE'S THE AUTO CLUB?

THE MODERN ROAD

Fittingly, the word Topanga refers to "where the mountain meets the sea." It can also refer to a "place above." The word is borrowed from the Tongva language. However, the root of the word comes from the Chumash language.

FROM THE VALLEY TO THE OCEAN

A Personal Note

My wife attended Canoga Park High School in the 1950s. The architecture reminded one of Tomas Jefferson's home at Monticello. There was no senior high school in Woodland Hills at the time. That would be later with Taft High School. She took a school bus, did quite well in her classes, and, following graduation, enrolled at UCLA. The tuition, by the way, was $50.00 per semester, and parking was free. It was there that she met the other man in her life, one William Shakespeare. He was a tough competitor for me with his sonnets and tragedies, as well as all the histories he wrote. What's a guy to do? I boned up on Othello, Henry IV, and that Prince from Denmark. The road to romance is not always easy, but it was enlightening.

A BEAUTIFUL SCHOOL

While at Westwood, she worked for Atomics International in Canoga Park. It was a well-paying part-time job in the aerospace industry. As an English major who used some of the first electric typewriters, she assisted the engineering geniuses with their writing. When we drive in the area, we can still see reminders of those days.

LET'S GO TO THE MOON

The streets were a little quieter in those days, as the following photo shows. This is Canoga Avenue in Woodland Hills between Victory and Ventura Boulevards. What was, as they say…

WHEN THE STREETS WERE LESS CONGESTED
IN WOODLAND HILLS

CHAPTER 21 – VAN NUYS

Van Nuys, California, its history, and its naming are tied to two men: Isaac Newton Van Nuys (1835-1912) and Isaac Lankershim (1818-1898). Van Nuys came from a farming family in upstate New York. Seeking other vistas, he moved to California. In 1866, he opened a general store in Napa Valley. It was there that he met Lankershim, a grain farmer at the time. Lankershim was in the process of buying over 59,000 acres in the San Fernando Valley from Pio Pico. Van Nuys decided to invest in the purchase. Unmarried, he moved to Los Angeles. There, and six years later, he married Lankershim's daughter. Her name was Susanna (1846-1923).

The two men did well growing wheat in the Valley. After Lankershim died in 1882, Van Nuys became involved in banking and real estate. Again, he did well. In 1908, he sold his ranch to developers. In 1909, the town of Van Nuys was named for him, even though W.P. Whitsett (1875-1965) was considered the true founder of the community. Van Nuys Boulevard was named after Isaac Van Nuys in 1926. It had originally been called Sherman Way.

VAN NUYS, LANKERSHIM, WHITSETTS

Sylvan Street in Van Nuys has a fascinating history. It was initially called Virginia Street. It was, however, renamed in 1917 by a city ordinance.

Again, it was the old problems. There already was a Virginia Avenue in Hollywood. The new name was supposed to be Marginia. However, other names were suggested, including Sylvan. That word means "wooded." There were, of course, very few wooded areas in the Van Nuys area. So, how did the name come about? One view is that the "Syl" comes from Sylmar Street and the "van" from Van Nuys. Might be… Naturally, there is still another unsubstantiated view. In 1917, the Sylvan Theater opened near the Washington Monument. This outdoor theater was a significant event and was featured in local newspapers. Did someone in Van Nuys take a liking to it? Hard to know…

Rubio Avenue in Van Nuys has a nice sound to it. It was so named in 1916. The street seems to be named after Ruby Hamilla Hay (1902-1979). She was the oldest daughter of William Hamilton Hay (1864-1946), who was a land developer. He is credited with subdividing the Encino area of California. His estate was called Hayvenhurst. Later, that would be a street in the Valley. Over time, he was involved in subdividing West Los Angeles and San Bernardino. He was also the founding member of the Los Angeles Athletic Club and a lifetime member of the Encino Chamber of Commerce.

His daughter, after attending UC Berkeley and earning a BA in 1924, worked as a librarian before marrying a history professor at UCLA. His name was John Whipple Olmsted (1903-1986). He was later hired to teach at UC Riverside. He was the university's first professor.

RUBY HAY, 1924, WILLIAM HAMILTON
HAY, JOHNWHIPPLE OLMSTED

What kind of name is "zombar?" Sounds like something made up. And that maybe the case… Zombar Avenue was named in 1927 on a piece of real estate owned by the Security Trust and Savings Bank. One of the bankers was a guy named John Henry Ramboz (1879-1960). He was a banker with the Merchants National Bank. There was also another banker named Sumpter F. Zombro (1864-1937). Both men were highly respected. You know… Prominent in financial circles… So was the name made up? Conjecture suggests the following. There already was a Ramboz Drive in Los Angeles. That couldn't be duplicated in the Valley. That being the case was an anagram created? Was Ramboz turned into Zombar? No one knows for sure.

John Henry Ramboz was an interesting fellow. In addition to being a banker, he also served as president of the Ambassador Hotel and as director of the Metropolitan Water District. As noted earlier, he was with Merchants National Bank, where he rose to the position of vice president after twenty-five years of faithful service. The president of the bank was William David Woolwine (1854-1927). He has a street named after him, Woolwine Drive, in the City of Terrence. It is one street over from Ramboz Drive. At the very least, there is a banking connection here.

JOHN H. RAMBOZ, WILLIAM DAVID WOOLWINE

A Personal Note

Van Nuys is dear to my heart. Here's why. Back in 1968, I decided marrying Jan would be a good thing. I proposed. She agreed. Now we needed rings. We drove over to Fedco, an early Wal-Mart that catered to government employees. Every ring was beyond our modest income, now combined. Finally, we found a ring selling for $25.00. For $50.00, we were in business. We put the rings on, and they haven't been off since that fateful day.

Van Nuys also provided me with three jobs, as it turns out. In the summer of 1963, I drove a school bus to a private summer school. Once I picked up 20 elementary school kids, I moved them to the camp. After depositing them, I changed into a swimsuit and pretended to teach them how to swim. I got a few bucks for all this, plus my free lunch. That's what teachers did in the old days. The following summer, I had a second summer job working in a sporting goods store, where I pretended to be an expert on guns. That really amounted to asking the customer, "What size buffalo was he going after?" The paperwork was relatively straightforward, and most customers appeared to be relatively sane at the time of the purchase. My last job in the area was in 1979. I was hired to teach at Van Nuys High School. I retired from the school district 20 years later, after a long stint as a dean.

VAN NUYS HIGH SCHOOL

In retirement, I joined the Van Nuys Kiwanis Club, which met at the Air-Tel Hotel. In time, I worked with three high school Key Clubs, including one at Van Nuys High. That was a nice avocation in retirement.

CHAPTER 22 – IN THE LIMELIGHT

The San Fernando Valley, as we have seen, was home to Spanish explorers and missionaries, as well as vast ranches deeded by the Spanish crown in Madrid. In turn, the Valley saw the introduction of grain and wheat farming under Spanish, Mexican, and Yankee farmers, as well as great herds of cattle to feed those who relished a good steak. Then came the citrus harvest of grapefruit, oranges, and lemons, all wonderful fruits to be exported eastward to those beyond the Mississippi River. It was expected, or so it seems, that businesses would ultimately thrive, along with small towns, once the railroads crossed the land. Then came the bankers, speculators, and developers, all seeking a return on their investments. Almost by its own violation, the land was sold and resold, eventually being subdivided into residential parcels.

A new word was added to the Valley's lexicon --- subdivision. And all that was dependent on one necessary resource, water from distant mountains for a semi-arid valley with a dearth of the substance of life. All this was marked by one word --- growth.

Given its proximity to Hollywood, the movie studios, and the home of magic on a screen, it was more than fortuitous that film stars, celebrities, if you will, would migrate to the Valley. With cash in hand and relatively inexpensive land available, many could purchase sizeable pieces of real estate for investment and secluded horse ranches. In a real sense, it was Hollywood in the sticks. Over time, some streets were named after expatriates from Los Angeles appropriately.

Bob Hope Drive in Burbank was, of course, named after the famed comedian and actor. This happened on his 86th birthday (1989). Burbank embraced Hope even though he lived in Toluca Lake, in a large home not far from the Lakeside Golf Club. Not bad for a guy who was born Leslie

Townes Hope in London, England. (1903-2003). Toluca Lake seemed suited to Hope. He and his wife, Dolores (1909-2011), lived in Toluca Lake for their entire lives.

Hope, of course, did well financially in the Hollywood biz. He, however, was also a businessman who made sound investments, including a most interesting one through his La Mancha Development Company. He bought and converted many shuttered Standard Oil gas stations into small shopping centers, which we would call mini malls. If the Valley is nothing else, it is undoubtedly the land of 7-Elevens, dry cleaners, laundry mats, and those who trim and paint mainly female nails.

BOB HOPE

Toluca Lake was subdivided out of the Forman Ranch in 1923. Apparently, the area was a muddy spring at the time. Developers cleaned up the unappetizing area. The first mention of Lake Toluca was in 1903, again at the Forman Ranch. The location was much more inviting by the time Hope made it his home.

Toluca has its origin in the word tollocan. That comes from the name of the god Tolo. When you had "can," the word denotes the "place of Tolo." In Aztec literature, it is referred to as Tolutepeti, meaning the god Tolo. It can also be an allusion to a volcano worshipped by the Aztecs.

———————————

A Personal Note

We all have our favorite Bob Hope movie. Who can forget all those "road" films that took us to Morocco, Rio, Zanzibar, and Singapore, even if we didn't leave a Hollywood back lot. Oh, I almost forgot… The Road to Bali and the Road to Utopia… All great fun… I think my favorites were, however, The Pale Face and The Son of Pale Face.

But my favorite moment with Hope was not in one of his movies. As a history teacher, I was fascinated by documentaries made during World War II. In one of those old black and white films, Hope is visiting G.I.s on some lonely Pacific island. During the war, he performed 79 shows throughout the South Pacific in July and August 1944.

BOB AND DOROTHY

On stage, before hundreds of sailors, Marines, and soldiers, he went into his usual one-person bit. At some point, Hope was joined by Dorothy Lamour. Turning to the defenders of democracy, he pointed to this Hollywood heartthrob and pulled the house down, saying, "Guys, I just wanted you to know what you're fighting for." No one could beat that line.

––––––––––

Tara Drive... You can probably guess where this name came from if, of course, you've seen *Gone with the Wind* (1939), starring Clark Gable (1901-1960) as the rogue, Rhett Butler. In real life, Gable had a 20-acre ranch located on Petit Avenue. However, he actually lived on Tara Drive in Encino. The house was called the "House of Two Gables." Why was this?

He lived there with his first wife, Carole Lombard (1908-1942). The ranch was subdivided in 1974 and was renamed the Clark Gable Ranch Estates. That was the same year Tara Drive was named in his honor. It was a cul-de-sac. Interestingly, there is another street nearby with a connection to the film's legacy. It is called Ashley Oaks because of the fictional character (Ashley Wilkes) played by Leslie Howard (1893-1943).

MOVIE STARS IN ENCINO

LESLIE HOWARD

THE BLOCKBUSTER

A Personal Note

I was born in 1939 in San Francisco. That was also the year, according to many film critics, when Hollywood had its greatest year. Of course, I was too young to appreciate this, nor did I have 23 cents for the average movie ticket. I had to wait a few years before I could see some of these films on television or at a theater celebrating their anniversary release. With the advent of DVDs, I snatched a few for personal viewing, including Stagecoach with John Wayne, Mr. Smith Goes to Washington with Henry Fonda, The Hunchback of Notre Dame with Charles Laughton, Goodbye, Mr. Chips with Greer Garson, and The Hound of the Baskervilles with Basil Rathbone. Talk about great films... And now I can stream them.

Cagney Street is in Granada Hills. For those of us who like a lively dancer, singer, and a guy who could play a tough guy, James Cagney (1899-1986) was your man. He owned a ranch in Granada Hills, which he purchased in 1953. It was called "Bull Canyon Meadows" at that time. A few years later, in 1964, Cagney sold about 450 acres to developers who wanted to construct residential units. That was also the year a street was named after him. Not a bad idea to name a street after the seller. Perhaps there was a discount involved. Who knows?

A street named after a former vaudeville player and a star in his own right, Cagney was featured in over fifty movies, including a favorite among American audiences, *Yankee Doodle Dandy* (1942). Other favorites of the movie-going public were *Angel with Dirty Faces* (1938), *The Roaring Twenties, White Heat* (1949), *Public Enemy* (191), and *Ragtime* (1981). That's quite a list.

THE ACTOR, THE FILM

No question about it… Walt Disney Drive in Encino is named after the creator of our favorite rodent, the beloved character Mickey Mouse, a love of children everywhere. Of course, that had to be Walter Elias Disney (1901-1966). This is a very private road just off Mulholland Drive. The street leads to the exclusive Curtis Elementary School, specifically to its parking lot. Apparently, one of the school's strongest supporters was Sharon Disney relative (1936-1993). She had a hand in naming the street.

Disney owned a few homes. One was in Holmby Hills, on Carolwood Drive. He wasn't the only star, so to speak, in the area. Both Frank Sinatra and Michael Jackson were neighbors. The street name appears to be related to Caroline Letts (1836-1912). Her son owned The Broadway department store. He also owned the land that eventually became Westwood and Holmby Hills.

That's a pretty good piece of property.

FOREVER, LONG GONE

A Personal Note

The Disney films were, as I am sure they were for you, a special part of our youth, and films we revisited with our own children, and now with our grandchildren. Three classics come immediately to mind: Pinocchio (1940), Bambi (1942), and Cinderella (1950). Other Disney films still resonate with us: Peter Pan (1953), Mary Poppins (1964), and Fantasia (1940). I, of course, and my personal favorites: Treasure Island (1950) and 20,000 Leagues Under the Sea (1954). Pirate treasure in one and creatures of the deep in the other... What fun and excitement. My children's favorites were always Pete's Dragon (1999) and The Rescuers (1977). Looking back, it's hard to imagine a childhood without all these Disney films.

––––––––––––

He has a street named after him in Jefferson Park. His name before finding his way to Hollywood was Edmund Lincoln Anderson (1905-1977). No problem if you don't recognize the name. How about a few hints? He was born into a family involved in the entertainment industry in Oakland, California. Eventually, he would make his mark in radio, film, and on television, his gravelly voice notwithstanding. He was adept at comedy and dance routines. Before he really hit it big, he had appeared in about thirty movies. Still nothing... Well, how about this... He was the wisecracking porter on the Jack Benny Show. Surely, you now know who we're talking about, one Eddie "Rochester" Anderson, Benny's foil on the show, where he was known as Rochester Van Jones. Who can forget his often-used famous line, "Mr. Benny, when will I get paid?"

Anderson lived on W. 37th Street in Los Angeles. Two years after his death, the cul-de-sac was renamed in his honor. That was in 1979. By that time, his popularity rivaled that of Benny, whose theatrical persona was that of a cheapskate, penurious with his money to say the least. Who can forget that favorite moment that brought tears of laughter to the radio audience?

Holdup Guy to Benny: "Your money or your life."
Benny to the holdup Guy: "I'm thinking. I'm thinking..."

At the time of his death, Anderson was the highest-paid black actor in the U.S. In his will, he stated that his home, which a black architect designed, should be converted into a halfway house for men struggling with addiction abuse.

THE MAN, THE TEAM

Her name was Mary Frances Reynolds (1932-2016). She was born in El Paso, Texas. Fortunately for her and the movie-going audience, her parents moved to Burbank in 1941. It was here that she was crowned Miss Burbank in 1948. In the same year, Warner Bros. signed Reynolds to a film contract. That led to a name change. She was renamed Debbie, and that's how we think of her. In time, she moved over to MGM, where she hit it big with *Singin' in the Rain* (1952).

Now, as to the street named after her... Initially, it was called Joaquin Drive in Burbank. That was changed to Debbie Reynolds Drive in 1971 to honor the favorite daughter of Burbank. Apparently, she wasn't involved in that decision. After intense lobbying by the Burbank City Council, the street was again renamed Joaquin. Reynolds went along with the Council's decision. That was in 1972. Then, in 1983, developers named a new connecting road Reynolds Drive.

THE GAL THE FILM

A Personal Note

Of course, Reynolds made other films, including three of my favorites: Meet Me in Las Vegas (1956), The Mating Game (1959), and How the West Was Won (1962). Okay, I'll admit it. I also liked The Unsinkable Molly Brown (1964). So, what's your favorite film with this charming actress?

Our last street is easy to pinpoint. DeMille Drive in Los Feliz is named after Cecil Blount de Mille (1881-1959). Spelling slightly differently, DeMille was his professional name). Early in Hollywood history, two men picked him to direct *The Squaw Man* in 1923. The two men were Jesse Lasky and Samuel Goldwyn, both later giants in the movie industry. Over the course of his career, DeMille would be involved in at least 70 screen features, including two memorable ones, *The Ten Commandments* (1956) and Union Pacific (1939)

THE DIRECTOR, OF THE PRODUCTION

THE EPIC

CHAPTER 23 – SUNLAND-TUJUNGA

Let's start at the beginning… What does Tujunga mean? The word can mean an "old woman's place," according to the Tongva language. The name can also refer to Mother Nature. A lovely meaning for a town in the Valley…

Ever hear of the Lemp Brewery of St. Louis? Probably not… And what does a Missouri company have to do with a street sign in Sun Valley? Well, let's see.

The brewery was established in 1840. The Griesedierck Beverage Company acquired the Lemp Brewery in 1920. Later, that company became the Falstaff Brewing Corporation. Keep all of that in mind.

Johann Adam Lemp was born in Germany in 1798. He arrived in the U.S. in 1936 and went into the grocery business in St. Louis. Over time, he realized that his store was more popular for its extensive beer selection than for its kitchen items. That being the case, he exited the grocery business and opened a brewery and saloon. Over time, his son, William J. Lemp, took over the company (1867-1922). The younger Lemp is credited with shipping lager beer by rail. Apparently, lager beer held up better to ship over great distances than most concoctions. We talked for 20 miles. This led to the advent of regional beer brands.

WILLIAM J. LEMP, THE PRODUCT

So was Lemp Avenue in Sun Valley named after a brewery? The evidence remains inconclusive. Did someone from St. Louis, but now living in the Valley, christen the street on behalf of a great beer in 1923? Could be. In any event, there is no connection between Lemp and Sun Valley. But… Since the 1850s, there has been a Lemp Avenue in St. Louis.

Klump Avenue is named after William Klump (1862-1944). He was born in Michigan to a German family. He moved to Los Angeles around 1890. It looks like he owned a farm south of the city limits. After marrying Maggie May Hoansler (1877-1957), the family moved to North Hollywood (which was then called Toluca). They grew apricots, peaches, and walnuts. The farm prospered, as did another business, banking. In 1910, he became the director at the Bank of Lankershim and gained prominence as a citizen of North Hollywood. To that end, the former Winifred Avenue was changed to Klump Avenue in 1924.

One wonders if Klump ever had a lager made by Lemp? It's fun to speculate.

THE KLUMPS, ORIGINAL BANK OF LANKERSHIM

Here's a question to keep you up at night? What does Samoa Street in Sun Valley have to do with a utopian farm community near San Ysidro and close to San Diego? And how did a guy by the name of Bolton Hall (1854-1938) influence another fellow by the name of William E. Smythe (1861-1922)? At first glance, nothing... But...

SMYTHE, HALL, THE BOOK

UTOPIA

Bolton Hall wrote a book entitled *A Little Land and a Living.* The theme was this. A group of families, working collectively, should till small farms of approximately one to five acres, sufficient to sustain a family. William E. Smythe, a writer and journalist, was inspired by Hall's writings. The first utopian colony was established on August 1, 1908, on the Bolton Ranch. It was named San Ysidro after the patron saint of farmers. In time, the concept spread to the San Fernando Valley. Ah, the plot thickens.

In 1913, a Little Landers Colony was established in the Sunland-Tujunga area. This was the culmination of Smythe and Marshall V. Hartranft's efforts, who is considered the "godfather" of Tujunga. The community's original name was Los Terrenitos. That's Spanish for *The Little Lands.* This led to the naming of a local street, San Ysidro Road, in reference to the San Diego colony.

In 1932, Tujunga was annexed by the City of Los Angeles, and duplicate street names had to be changed to avoid postal service conflicts. Herein was the problem. There already was a San Ysidro Drive in Benedict Canyon. That's when an unknown civil servant chose a replacement name. Samoa Street got the nod. No one is sure why. One view is that Samoa begins "Sa," and so does San Ysidro. Was that what happened? Does it really matter? The hidden history is what drives our interest: a utopian Shangri-La in Sunland-Tujunga.

Today, you can visit Bolton Hall, which was the community center for the utopian project. It was built in 1913. Today, the building is the Bolton Hall Historical Museum. It opened in 1980. Visitors are welcome every Sunday and Tuesday. No admission. Sounds like a good deal if you're interested in history.

BOLTON HALL

All of us enjoy a hike now and then, especially if it's a path leading a wayward city dweller up a mountainside with vista views with every step. Indeed, that's a nice way to get away from the humdrum of daily life. You know, work, sleep, eat, catch the daily news, figure out if the kids did their homework, and then wonder if the boss liked your presentation. It's so lovely to be on that mountain, especially if it's called Mount Gleason, located in the Angeles National Forest just south of Soledad Canyon in the Sylmar area. At the summit, the mountain stands at 6,530 feet, a steep climb that usually takes a few hours.

For those who like history... The mountain is named after George Gleason (1839-1926), as is the street in Sunland-Tujunga that bears his name. It received its current name, Mount Gleason Avenue, in 1929 after replacing the former name, Walnut Avenue.

ESCAPE

So what's the story on George Gleason? A few facts... He was born in Connecticut and spent a few years at sea before joining the Confederate Army during the American Civil War. How a Yankee came to do that is an open question. He arrived in California in 1863 and entered the mining business in the area now known as Soledad Canyon, located on the north side of the San Gabriel Mountains. He mined for gold and quartz. Reports of the day describe his efforts to bring down timber from the mountain to shore up his mine. In 1873, the hill was named Mount Gleason after him due to his mining activities.

MINING ON THE MOUNTAIN

In 1887, a post office was established in the town of Monte Vista. Today, we refer to the area as Sunland in deference to the beautiful Mediterranean climate for which Southern California is renowned. Soon afterwards, Sunland Boulevard was named after it replaced Hansen

Street. That was in 1929. Hansen Street was named after Dr. Homer Alfred Hansen (1872-1960). The street was on his Hansen Heights tract. The good doctor was from Logan, Ohio. In California, he excelled as a physician and, even better, it seems, in land development. One of his investments was tied to the development of Thousand Oaks (1922). Hansen Dam was built on Dr. Hansen's property. It was dedicated in 1940.

THE DOCTOR, THE DAM

It began as Manzanita Street. In 1929, the name was changed to McGroarty Street to honor John Steven McGroarty (1862-1944. It's fair to ask, who was this man? The simple answer is this. He was a person of renown. He was a two-term congressman (1935-1939). He was a published biographer and historian. He practiced his writing skills as a columnist for the *Los Angeles Times*. He was also California's poet laureate. That's quite a resume.

McGroarty and his wife, Ida (1866-1940), came from the Quaker State, with a brief stop in Montana, before settling in California. They built a home in Tujunga. It was called "Rancho Chupa Rosa, which seems to mean hummingbird or hummingbird bush in Spanish. Of course, it can also refer to a flowering shrub that attracts hummingbirds. Today, the home is the McGroarty Art Center, the birds notwithstanding.

This literate man was best known for writing the *Mission Play*. It was a romanticized historical epic about the California missions. It is reportedly staged over 3,200 times. His wife designed the sets and costumes. The play was first staged in San Gabriel in 1920. By 1944, over 2.5 million people had seen it. The play was described as a three-hour pageant.

THE TEAM, THE PLAY

In the second act of the play, Father Junipero Sierra, now bent and old, kneels before a great Cross to pray. What leaves his lips is a prayer for all Californians, then and now.

"Hear, O Lord, thy servant whose days upon the earth are about to close... Please bring to the foot of thy cross these wild Gentiles of the plains and hills. Bless this dear land of California, and all its people--- now, and in the centuries to come. This is the prayer of thy servant, Junipero, who is old and worn, and who must soon say 'Farewell.'"

MISSION SAN GABRIEL

THE PLAY – SOLDIERS, PRIESTS, AND NATIVE PEOPLE

CHAPTER 24 – BURBANK

Burbank has many street signs of interest, none more notable than Burbank Boulevard, which was once called Central Avenue before receiving a well-deserved name change. The whole business began with Dr. David Burbank (1821-1895). Born in New Hampshire and trained as a dentist, he moved to San Francisco just after the mad "gold rush." That was in 1854. Over time, he and his wife moved to Los Angeles, where he continued his practice. Pulling teeth and caring for dental challenges was lucrative, but in 1867, the good dentist found another, more profitable venture. In that year, he bought 4,600 acres of Rancho San Rafael and an additional 4,600 acres from Rancho La Providencia. On his large ranch, he hit it big, raising sheep and wheat. Given that he shuttered his dental practice in 1872. A few years later, he sold most of his holdings for $275,000. Providencia Land, Water Development Company purchased the land. One of its shareholders was, as might be expected, Dr. Burbank. The company established the town of Burbank in 1887, a year after acquiring the real estate.

DR. DAVID BURBANK

Hollywood Way... If you live in the west end of the Valley, you've probably taken this road on the way to Burbank Airport (Bob Hope Airport for some). First, you jumped on the 118 (Ronald Reagan Interstate) before leaning to the south and joining the I-5 until you reach Hollywood

Way. Probably, you never gave thought to how the name came about, except for its proximity to the movie studios. So what's the story?

A land developer is credited with naming Hollywood Way. His name was Earl Loy White (1885-1971). Along with his wife, he came west from Kansas. Once in the Southland, he bought a dairy farm in rural Burbank, near the intersection of Verdugo and Pioneer avenues.

Verdugo, by the way, means "executioner." That makes no sense unless Jose Maria Verdugo (1751-1831) was just that as a Spanish-Mexican soldier. The historical records do not indicate that he was a hangman. Indeed, he was a corporal of the guard at Mission San Gabriel. For his service, he was granted over 36,000 acres comprising Rancho San Rafael. Today's map indicates land holdings that include the Verdugo Mountains, from San Fernando to Pasadena. Nice perk...

On November 23, 1924, Pioneer Avenue was renamed Hollywood Way. Apparently, it did so to great fanfare. White was a driving force behind this change. He wanted movie people to shuttle between Hollywood and the Magnolia Park subdivision. How much influence? When the City of Burbank didn't want to fund the work, White used his own money to grade the road. Eventually, the Hollywood Way would extend from San Fernando Road to Cahuenga Pass. It appears that Burbank reimbursed White. Ah, civility in both directions.

White had a hand in the development of Magnolia Park and the naming of Screenland Drive within the project. Perhaps he hoped, as some think, to lure the movie industry into the area, or at least those who worked for the studios.

WHITE PROMOTES THE NEW ROAD

Buena Vista Street is always associated with Walt Disney. That's understandable since the headquarters for Walt Disney Studios were on the street. The street name was on the books as of 1916, but it wasn't named for Mickey's creator. Someone in the Burbank bureaucracy did it. The name means "good view" in Spanish.

Disney's studios had been on Hyperion Avenue in Burbank until 1939. Following the success of *Snow White and the Seven Dwarfs* and its strong box office, the studio relocated to Buena Vista Street. As to Hyperion... He was one of the Titans of Greek mythology and, if you want to know, the father of Helios, the god of the sun. Perhaps that's why the street was so named, being, as it was, in sunny California. Another possibility for the street laid out in 1887 might refer to Henry Wadsworth Longfellow's *Hyperion,* written in 1846. Might just be.

LONGFELLOW, HYPERION

Although not a mainstay in our public schools, the poet's lyrics contain words that enrich our lives.

"...every heart has its secret sorrows, which the world knows not, and oftentimes we call a man cold, when he is only sad."

And...

"Look not mournfully into the Past. It does not come back again. Wisely improve the Present. It is time. Go forth to meet the shadow Future, without fear and with a manly heart."

There is no university in Burbank. In nearby Glendale, there is a community college. At one time, however, one man tried to create a university community in Burbank. His name was Benjamin Walter Marks (1883-1946). The story begins in 1919. In that year, he planned a subdivision named Woodland Heights. His vision included something similar to today's Westwood, the lively home of UCLA. Within a 5,000-acre city-within-a-city, he sought to establish a campus, a home for the new UC branch in Los Angeles. As part of his plan, there would be a hotel, a country club, a finishing school for women, and a military academy for boys. Hundreds of residential units would emerge around the university campus. Talk about thinking big.

THE VISION

A great road would thread its way through this development. He named it University Avenue. In 1929, the UC Regents rejected his proposal and moved the Bruins from their original location on Normal Avenue in East Hollywood to Westwood. That was it. The dream was over.

Trivia… In the past, almost any college offering post-high school degrees in education was referred to as a regular school. At Vermont and Normal Avenue, the UCLA campus bristled with students. Initially, the school was known as the Los Angeles State Normal School. That was back in 1913. Six years later, it was incorporated into the UC system as a teacher college. In 1927, the school was officially renamed UCLA. In 1938, the Vermont campus got a new lease on life. It was reincarnated as Los Angeles Junior College. Nice…

Burbank has several streets named after universities and colleges, including Amherst Drive, Andover Drive, and UCLAN Drive. This is higher education on street signs.

Amherst Drive in Burbank was named in 1920 as part of the Woodland Heights development. Bethany Road honored Bethany College in Kansas. Cornell Drive spoke to another college, as did Delaware Road (University of Delaware). There was also Elmhurst Drive, named for Elmhurst University in Illinois. And then there was Fairmount Road for a college of the same name. You know the school today as Wichita State. Of course, Grinnell Drive for the school in Iowa…

A Personal Note…

Naturally, I'm biased toward Uclan Drive, another street in Burbank. How could I not be? My wife got her MA in English there. I completed my doctorate program in education a bit later. Anyway, as you know, UCLA students were once called "Uclans." Today, of course, they are known as Bruins." The street was named in 1951 to be one of the community's college-themed streets. A couple of land developers were involved in all this: Edward K. Zuckerman (1908-1981) and Barney R. Morris (1909-1985). Both were UCLA alums. That said, it's time for the UCLA fight song.

We are the mighty Bruins
The best team in the West
We're marching on to victory
To conquer all the rest

We are the mighty Bruins
Triumphant evermore
You can hear from far and near
The Mighty Bruin roar!

Stagg Street in Burbank, let's be clear, was not named after a bunch of party guys. The honor goes to Amos A. Stagg (1862-1965), who is sometimes known as the "grand old man of football" for his playing and coaching exploits at the University of Chicago. So important was Stagg to football that schools and playing fields were named after him across the country. Was some anonymous civil engineer aware of Stagg's history? If he read the sports section, he had to be. At least that's one theory.

RETIREMENT OF A LEGEND

Check out the mug shot below. It was taken in 1932. That's a guy named Isaac Rohrer Landis (1883-1949).

Landis was later known as a "grafter," which is a con artist. You know, someone who swindles dopes out of their money through fraud. Other names apply to such folks—chiselers, scammers, and flim-flam men.

The title fit Landis. For example, in 1932, he was sentenced to four years at San Quentin—the charge: selling shares in a Lake Arrowhead property and pocketing the dough. In 1908, he was accused of swindling thousands of dollars from the good citizens of Whittier. He posed as the nephew of a famous judge while selling shares in a mining interest. Apparently, there was nothing on the mind. He was caught in Caliente, Naveda, while fleeing to Chicago. Even earlier in his nefarious life, he was the general manager of the Empire China Company, which operated in Burbank. Landis and his partner, Fred E. Keeler, owned a kaolin clay pit near Caliente, Nevada. The pit supplied the raw material needed to make porcelain and delicate China dishware. Within the company, he was associated with questionable bookkeeping practices.

That's the guy's resume. This brings us to a question. Why was a street named after him? No one seems to know. Of course, some would argue that, alongside land developers, bankers, and real estate types, good old Landis was in good company. That is, as it must be, a matter of opinion. Still, it's kind of nice to have a little wickedness on a street sign.

Okay, who was Los Angeles' first director of city planning? The answer is George Gordon Whitnall (1888-1977). Fittingly, it's assumed, a road bearing his name was appropriate. Whitnall Highway, which runs through Burbank and North Hollywood, bears its legacy. Again, the fundamental question… Who was this man?

His family left Wisconsin for Los Angeles in 1911. His parents, it should be noted, were Socialists in both ideas and practice, at least as they viewed government and its role in people's lives. Gordon, as it liked to be called, quickly became the spokesman for the local Socialist Party. Two years later, he challenged the uncontrolled growth of Los Angeles. He wasn't against growth. He just wanted a rational system by which the city could grow. He helped establish the City Planning Association. This was a civic organization with a significant goal: proper zoning should translate into sensible growth. In time, this organization evolved into the Department of City Planning. That was in 1920. As it turns out, Gordon was asked to head the agency and served in that role for a decade. In his speeches with developers, he won a few and lost even more, but he did try to bring some rationality to the process. After retiring, he served as a private consultant to the city, while also teaching urban planning at USC. Next time you're on Whitnall Highway, give a quiet yell to old Gordon.

THE CITY PLANNER

CHAPTER 25 – GLENDALE

Those who take the air are used to flying out of LAX or Burbank Airport. But in 1929, that wasn't the case. At that time, you entered Glendale's Grand Central Air Terminal by way of Air Way, which was the entry road to the runways. A perfect name for a road to an airfield, wouldn't you say? The airport would last until 1959. At that time, it was transformed into Grand Central Avenue. That's called progress, some would say. Still, there was a legacy to be found here. It began with Charles Clyde "C.C." Spicer (1878-1959). He had been a WWI fighter pilot.

He envisioned a commercial airport for the Valley even before Van Nuys Airport was established. In any event, Grand Central couldn't keep up with post-war traffic or the facilities needed for larger airplanes. Its chief competitor was Mines Field, which became Los Angeles Municipal Airport. Today it's called LAX. That's the story of Air Way.

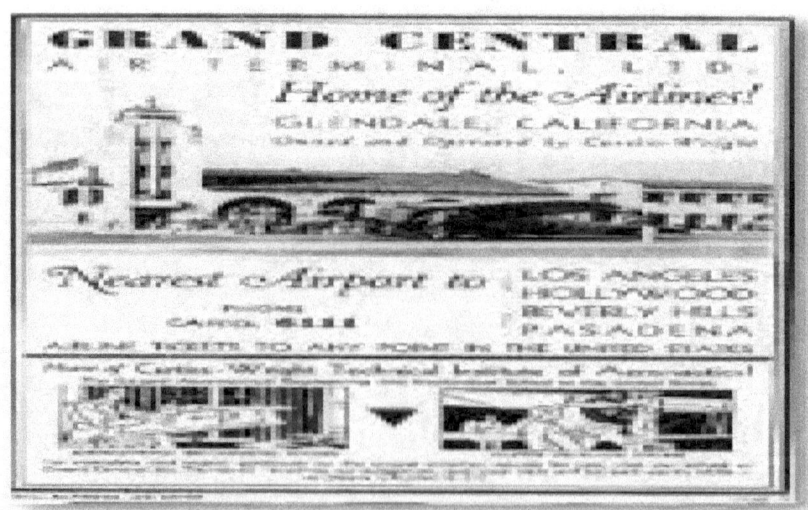

THE OLD TERMINAL

Many people flew in and out of the old airport. Perhaps the most famous was Amelia Earhart, the woman who set numerous air records and mysteriously disappeared somewhere in the Central Pacific while attempting to circumnavigate the world with her navigator, Fred Noonan. That was in 1937. The best guess is that her plane ran out of gas near Howland Island after her last known stop in Lae, New Guinea.

PREPARING FOR THE LAST FLIGHT

Death brought numerous eulogies, some in poetry, others in music. One to be recalled came out of the Bluegrass country... It was called Amelia Earhart.

> *'Twas a ship out on the ocean*
> *Just a speck against the sky*
> *Amelia Earhart was flying out that day.*
> *With her partner, Captain Newman, on the 2nd of July*
> *Her plane fell into the ocean far away.*
>
> *There's a beautiful, beautiful field*
> *Far away in a fair land*
> *Happy landings to you, Amelia Earhart*
> *Farewell, first lady of the air.*
>
> *Well, half an hour later, an SOS was heard*
> *The signal was weak, but still the voice was brave*
> *We prayed that she might fly home safe again.*
> *Tho in years to come others blazed a trail across the sea*
> *We'll never forget America and her plane.*

It should be noted that she was the first woman to fly across the Atlantic Ocean in 1928. She was a passenger on the plane. The pilot was Wilmer Stultz. The flight took 20 hours and 40 minutes to complete. In 1932, she made the flight on her own, and it took only 14 hours and 56 minutes. She carried with her a newspaper dated November 20, 1932, to confirm the date of her flight. After landing in a pasture north of Derry, Northern Ireland, she was asked by a native, "Have you flown far?" Her reply was on point: "From America."

In January 1887, Glendale Avenue was named, thereby becoming one of the first streets in the area. And, of the records, there was no Glendale at the time. People, yes. Businesses, yes... A Glendale, no... The city was initially called Riverdale. That was back in 1882. Apparently, there was a subdivision called that. In 1885, the name was replaced by its current moniker, but not easily.

The USPO stepped into the picture, arguing that the name needed to be dropped. Why, you ask? There was already a locale in Colorado with that name. Colorado! That's a different state. How could that happen? In the 1880s, the Post Office held immense power over site naming. In 1886, the postal folks settled on the name Mason. The community's residents didn't like it and didn't use it in their transactions. By 1891, it had gone the way of all tarnished street signs. Glendale stuck. By the way, Glendale refers to glen (a narrow valley) and dale (a broad valley).

There's a library in Glendale with an unusual name, El Miradero/ Brand Library. It's a converted house, really a mansion constructed by Leslie Brand (1871-1945) and his wife, Mary Louise (1859-1925). Both Brand and his wife would have streets honoring them. That was in 1904. El Miradero Avenue would take its name from the home where they lived. That occurred in 1926. The impulse for the structure, some say, was due to the 1893 World's Fair in Chicago. One of the exhibits was an Indian Pavilion.

EL MIRADERO/BRAND LIBRARY

The house was eventually deeded to the City of Glendale. In 1956, it was converted into a library, a significant project. This brings us to a question. What does Miradero mean? It refers to a viewpoint in Spanish or possibly a lookout. That seems to work, given the size of Brands' estate, which is some 800 acres in Glendale, including a private airfield for personal use.

LOUISE, BRAND

What could a ditch have to do with a street name, La Zanja Drive in Glendale? To begin... Zanja is a Spanish word for a ditch that carries water, sometimes for personal use and sometimes for irrigation. At one time, there were miles of small zanjas that brought water to plants and people in early Los Angeles. Zanjas, something more than muddy trenches, were often constructed with brick and concrete. The original ditch was called Zanja Madre or "Mother Ditch) during the early Spanish days in Los Angeles. The first ditch was open to the elements. This ditch diverted water from the L.A. River (Rio Porciuncula) to families and farms.

Believe it or not, many of the ditches were in use for almost 100 years. What ended their use? On the recommendation of William Mulholland, the ditches were covered up by 1904. They weren't as helpful and sanitary as underground pipes.

A FORMER ZANJA

IN SPANISH DAYS

Margaret Wolfe Hungerford (1855 -1897... Ever hear of her? In 1883, she published a romance novel. She did so under her pen name, which was "The Duchess." It was entitled *Rossmoyne*. At that time, Erskine Mayo Ross (1845-1928) owned between 700 and 1,100 acres in the Glendale area. The exact number of acres is in dispute. What is known is that, along with his wife, Inez Ross (1853-1907), he ran a ranch that flourished, growing fruit and olive trees. Erskine Ross was an attorney and judge before turning to ranching. He also cofounded Glendale in 1887.

Was Rossmoyne Avenue named after Ross? Could be. Or did it honor a romance novel, which caught their attention? The book came out in 1883. That was the same year the Ross ranch was named. A coincidence? Hard to know, that's for sure. In 1923, Rossmoyne Avenue was officially named on the Rossmoyne tract, which was part of the former ranch.

THE DUCHESS, ROSS

A GLENDALE STREET SIGN

Campbell Street in Glendale was named in 1904. It honors Daniel Campbell (1872-1932), who played a significant role in the city's growth. He was born in Ireland and later moved to the United States. In 1894, he joined the stampede for gold in the Yukon. Nothing like the Klondike Gold Rush to attract those seeking wealth in the streams and mountains of Alaska… Apparently, he did okay. Digging into the earth paid off for him. While in the Yukon, he met Joseph Brand (1868-1913). His brother was Leslie C. Brand of Glendale fame.

SEEKING GOLD IN THE YUKON

THE HARD WORK

In a long poem entitled The Spell of the Yukon Robert Service immortalized the trek to the Yukon and the lure of gold. The lines still enchant us.

> *I wanted the gold, and I sought it;*
> *I scrabbled and mucked like a slave.*
> *Was it famine or scurvy---I fought it;*
> *I hurled my youth into a grave.*
> *I wanted the gold, and I got it---*
> *Came out with a fortune last fall---*
> *Yet somehow life's not what I thought,*
> *And somehow the gold isn't all.*

> *No! There's the land (Have you seen it?)*
> *It's the cussedest land that I know.*
> *From the big, dizzy mountains that screen it*
> *To the deep, deathlike valleys below.*
> *Some say God was tired when He made it.*
> *Some say it's a fine land to shun;*
> *Maybe, but some would trade it*
> *For no land on earth ---and I'm one.*

Leaving the frozen north for sunnier haunts, Campbell came to L.A. It was there that Leslie Brand appointed the young Irishman to head the first bank in Glendale. Again, the prospector from Ireland did well. He eventually married Margaret McPeak around 1900, and they settled into their home in Glendale. They called it Ard Eevin. A local architect designed the house. His name was Nathaniel Dryden (1849-1924). It turns out there is an Ard Eevin Avenue in Glendale. It was so named in 1923. In Gaelic, Ard Eevin means "beautiful heights." As it turns out, there are two towns in Ireland called Ardeevin. Curious.

There is also a Dryden Street in Glendale. It was named, of course, for the architect, Nathaniel Dryden (1849-1924). The street was named after him in 1904. It appears that Leslie Brand was naming streets after those in his inner circle and acquaintances he admired. Dryden also designed the Virginia Robinson Estate in Beverly Hills in 1911. The heirs to the

Robinson Department store lived in the 12 rooms of the mansion, which cost $25,000 at the time.

ROBINSON DEPARTMENT STORE 1915

Grange Street in Glendale is not named after any person associated with the area. It was not even picked by a civil engineer hired by the city. According to legend and lore, there was a street on a tract map without a name. A co-worker noticed this. His name was Ralph Goodman. It turns out he was a football fan. He scribbled in the word "Grange." The City Council approved the name without debate. That was in 1915.

So, of course, who was the street named after? One possibility... Football fans know him as the "Galloping Ghost" for his exploits on the turf while playing for the "Fighting Illini of the University of Illinois football teams in the 1920s. His real name was Harold Edward "Red" Grange (1903-1991). At the time, he was one of the most famous athletes in America.

THE GALLOPING GHOST

How did Grange get his name? Two sports writers were involved: Grantland Rice and Warren Brown. Rice poetically described Grange in one of his columns.

> *A streak of fire, a breath of flame*
> *Eluding all who reach and clutch;*
> *A gray ghost thrown into the game*
> *The rival hands may never touch.*
> *A rubber-bounding, blasting soul*
> *Whose destination is the goal…*

A Chicago sportswriter picked up on the column and nicknamed Grange "The Galloping Ghost." That was Warren Brown.

OCTOBER 6, 1925

CHAPTER 26 – TOLUCA LAKE

Two questions challenge us immediately. First, who named Toluca Lake? Second, who named Toluca Lake Avenue? The answer to both questions is a bit confusing.

There is, of course, a city in Mexico called Toluca. There is also a volcanic mountain near the town that rises 15,020 feet into the sky. The origin of the name is from the word "tollocan." That refers to the god, Tolo, or "the place of Tolo." It can also be related to "the hill of the god." Apparently, the word began with the Aztecs after they took control of the area in 1473. Once under Spanish hands, starting in 1521, the city was called Toluca de San José.

NEVADO de TOLUCA

There was a Toluca Street in downtown Los Angeles, at least in 1888. No one is sure how it migrated to the Valley. But there were some signs… The Lankershim School District was changed to the Toluca School District. That was in 1892. A year later, the Toluca post office existed. And then…

Toluca was renamed Lankershim in 1907. In 1927, it was called North Hollywood. That's when Charles Forman got involved (1835-1818). He was involved with the Toluca Ranch. In 1903, there was mention of Lake Toluca on the ranch. Apparently, there was a stream on the ranch, a rather muddy one. A swamp perhaps... In 1923, the ranch was subdivided. Its new name was Toluca Lake Park. Looks like that became Toluca Lake. Toluca, by the way, means "fertile valley."

A TOLUCA LAKE PARK AD

As would be expected, there is a Forman Avenue in Toluca Lake. The man played a significant role in founding the town. His name replaced Laguna Avenue, which was one of the first streets in the Valley.

CHARLES FORMAN AND HIS RESIDENCE

Another street sign… This time Satsuma Avenue in Toluca Lake… As always, there's a story. This time it revolves around a plum, to be exact, the Satsuma plus. You got it right; the red, somewhat fleshy one is the one you pick up at Vons, along with bananas, apples, and oranges. And yes, there are streets somewhere in America named after apples and oranges, so why not one honoring the humble plum and a guy by the name of Carl Alfred Frieburg (1866-1936).

THE SATSUMA PLUM

He was of Swedish descent, a Scandinavian who arrived in Toluca Lake in 1891. He found a job managing Charles Forman's fruit orchards and later moved out onto the 65 acres he owned. According to government records, he controlled a tract that would later include Satsuma Avenue, named, of course, for the plums he was cultivating.

As to the meaning of the word… Satsuma refers to any cultivated and cold-tolerant mandarin tree that bears a medium-sized and essentially seedless fruit with a smooth skin. That's according to the dictionary. It can also refer to a variety of tangerines with loose skin. The word is also related to the former province of Japan. In Spanish, the word is Satsuman for a small orange fruit. Somehow, all of this is tied to a street sign in Toluca Lake.

A last point… Many local civic leaders wanted to name a street after Frieburg. He resisted. He suggested an alternative name for the street in question, which was located near Satsuma Avenue. The street is known today as Valley Spring Street.

WHEN IT WAS AGRICULTURAL

Speaking of fruit growers… Blix Street in Toluca Lake pays homage to Carl Anton Gustav Blix (1856-1928) and his family. He owned some 50 acres, some of which was where Blix Street now exists. He grew apricots, peaches, and plums. One of his daughters was Katie Blix (1895-1990). She spent her lifetime in the area with a most unusual avocation. For some sixty years, she voluntarily measured rainfall in the Valley, providing valuable data to local authorities. Most of that was before the Weather Channel.

KATIE BLIX

Vineland Avenue… What a nice name for a street, almost poetic in sound. The name first appeared on a subdivision map in 1887. At that time, it was on land controlled by the Lankershim Ranch and Water Company. The company controlled a significant amount, approximately 12,000 acres. On the subdivision map, Vineland was merely a pencil line before it evolved into a challenging dirt road. That didn't occur until 1911. The eventual name referred to "vineyards," which existed in Southern California at the time. It appears that other towns in the area emulated the vineyards, such as Beaumont in Riverside County and Baldwin Park in the San Gabriel Valley.

BURBANK 1928 – PICKING GRAPES

With the implementation of America's misguided effort to make the country "dry" during prohibition, at least one question emerged. What would happen to all the grapes? How would they be used? One answer was tied to a namesake in the supermarket. The Welch company was established in Vineland, New Jersey, in 1869. It was incorporated in 1893 and is known for its popular "Welch's Grape Juice." Did the company buy up all those grapes intended for a nice bottle of wine? At least much of the supply, that's for sure... The temperance movement certainly encouraged the popularity of grape juice. Before the prohibition, at least two government officials of some stature weighed in on the issue. William Jennings Bryan was the Secretary of State in 1913. He only served grape juice during formal diplomatic functions. The Secretary of War at the time was Josephus Daniels. He forbade any alcoholic drinks on board the country's naval ships. Booze was replaced with grapes in this man's navy.

As an aside...

What did Albert Einstein say about the issue?

Nothing is more destructive of respect for the government and the law of the land than passing laws that cannot be enforced.

What did Abraham Lincoln say about such laws?

Prohibition will cause significant injury to the cause of temperance. It is a species of intemperance within itself, for it goes beyond the bounds of reason, in that it attempts to control a man's appetite by legislation and in making crimes out of things that are not crimes.

A Personal Note

While teaching at Nobel Junior High in Northridge, I needed an additional job to supplement my lavish pay from the school district. To that end, I got a job in a liquor store on Reseda, just a short street down from Nordhoff, and only a few minutes from the school. The school bell rang at 3:00 p.m. By 3:30, I was waiting on customers. It was a quick leap, if not a seamless one, from discussing the Westward Movement to the world of Jim Beam, Smirnoff Vodka, and Gordon's Gin. Anything for a buck, as you can see. My principal found out about my extra hours activities and called me into his office. He felt it was unbecoming for a man to work in a liquor store. "What would happen if the parents of my students knew this?" he asked. "Not much," I responded. "Indeed, I often discuss a student's progress with a parent making a purchase." His only response fell short of what was expected. "Well, it's not very professional." I answered, "Perhaps not, but nor is my paycheck

CHAPTER 27 – STUDIO CITY

Studio City is named after the movie studio lot established by Mack Sennett in 1927. Land developers provided Sennett with 20 acres of land. It was the height of silent films, featuring the antics of the Keystone Kops. Over time, the Mack Sennett Studios evolved into Republic Pictures. That studio is now known as Radford Studio Center. In the past, the area was part of Rancho Ex-Mission San Fernando.

SENNETT AND HIS STUDIO

KEYSTONE KOPS

Bakman Avenue is named after the Bakman family, a clan from Ohio that settled in the Toluca area in the 1880s. One member of the family was Dan Bakman (1877-1932). He prospered in banking, becoming a partner at the Bank of Lankershim. He also did well in real estate. He is credited with being the driving force behind the development of Riverside Drive. So far, so good…

Every family has a secret or a hidden past. Some more than one… In this case, the culprit was Daniel Frederick Bakman (1898-1939). He didn't rob a bank. He didn't steal money from clients. Nope, he was a bit more violent than that. In 1930, full of rage, he killed his wife's lover. He blew the guy away with a full shotgun blast to the abdomen in a spot called Dark Canyon. Today, it is known as Barham Boulevard in North Hollywood. Justice was served. Good old Daniel was convicted of manslaughter and sent to San Quentin. That should have been the end of his violent career. It wasn't. He was released from the "Big House" in 1936. Soon after, he kidnapped and assaulted a North Hollywood woman, which got him a free ticket to Folsom Prison up near Sacramento. Something unusual occurred. He had a heart attack, some say. He also took a 15-foot plunge into the prison quarry. Either way, he was kaput.

1930 MUG SHOT

Sometimes names can be confusing, as in the case of Bakman and Bakeman. A bit of trivia…

Daniel Frederick Bakeman was born in 1759. He died in 1869. His claim to fame was this. He was the last soldier from the Revolutionary War to receive a pension from the government for his service in the rebellion. He was 106 years old when he cashed it in. He was buried in Cattaraugus County in New York State in the small town of Freedom. It seems that someone in the planning department was aware of this.

THE LAST SOLDIER

Some street signs are alive with history, hidden from those who walk past them. But if Colfax Avenue could talk, oh what it might say.

Schuyler Colfax (1823-1885) was an Indiana politician. He was the Speaker of the House of Representatives during the presidency of Abraham Lincoln. He was the Vice President of the United States under President Ulysses S. Grant. He trekked through the West, seeking agricultural and mining opportunities to help fund the Union cause and the later "reconstruction" of the nation. Pretty neat stuff for a Hoosier…

Colfax was honored with a street in 1917. At the time, there were already two spots bearing his name. The longest commercial street in the country was in Denver. That was one. The other was the small town of Colfax in Northern California. Did the civil engineers in Los Angeles know about these spots and his service to the country? Probably. Is that why a street was named for him? Possibly. Colfax Avenue actually replaced Eucalyptus Avenue. That was until 1915, when the City of Los Angeles annexed the Valley. Guess what? There was already an Eucalyptus Street in the city. One had to go. The Valley's lost or gain? It all depends on how you look at it.

THE ELECTION OF 1868

The man had a way with words. For example:

These martyrs of patriotism gave their lives for an idea.

Let us have faith that Right makes Might; and in that faith, let us, to the end, dare to do our Duty.

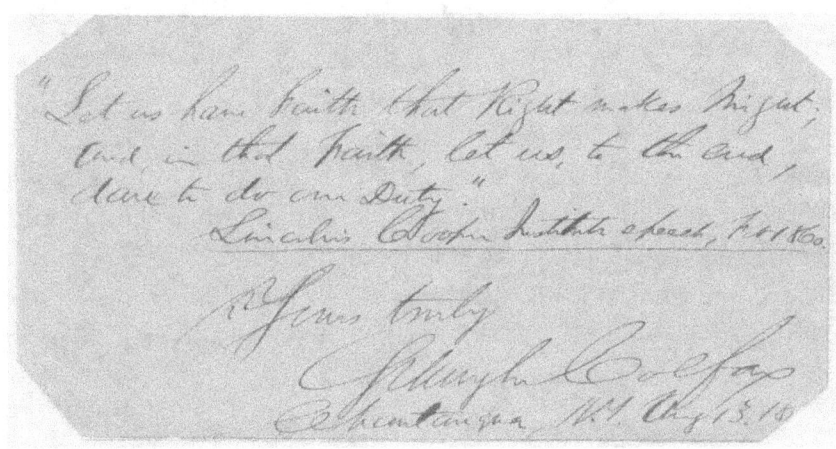

An aside… Imagine the confusion that never occurred. In 1967, an attempt was made to name a street after Sandy Koufax, the Los Angeles Dodger "hall of fame" pitcher. Members of the City Council wanted to rename Fairfax Avenue after the fire-throwing hauler. The effort struck out. There was reluctance to name streets after anyone still living. Too bad… Colfax and Koufax… What fun…Hopefully, a street will be named for him in the future. A proposal… Carve out a short street in the parking lot at Dodger Stadium for this Dodger great. Call if Koufax Way. If that happens, throw in one for Don Drysdale. That makes for a great tandem.

KOUFAX AND DRYSDALE

In 1923, a parcel of land was sold in what is now Studio City. The seller was David G. Maxwell (1861-1939). He was also known as "Uncle Dave." After the sale, he named Maxwellton Road after his family. He was from Chicago, where he made his wealth as the owner of a box manufacturing company. Along with his wife, Mary (1865-1941), he also bred champion Holsteins in Waterloo, Iowa.

UNCLE DAVE AND HIS HOLSTEINS

In 1920, the couple relocated to Los Angeles, bringing with them 160 cows. They bought a 263-acre dairy farm for their proposed "livestock showplace." As they did so, they experienced the rapid growth of the Valley. Land, it appears, was more valuable than cows. The livestock was sold off, and the property was subdivided. The couple then moved to Beverly Hills.

Uncle Dave made the papers in 1925. Dr. Jean Paul Fernel, who was a Chicago plastic surgeon, sued him for $1,000,000. What was this all about? Fernel claimed that Maxwell had hijacked the affection of his young wife. Her name was Ruth. It appears the case was settled quietly or just dismissed. As to Dr. Fernel... He was, according to many accounts, a quack with a long-as-your-arm criminal record. He eventually ended up in jail for selling bogus breast reduction pills. The Maxwell marriage, it should be noted, survived all this.

Radford Avenue is named after Joseph D. Radford (1857-1918). It replaced Plater Avenue. The designation was appropriate. Mayor Frederic Woodman (1872-1949) did the honor in 1918.

RADFORD AND WOODMAN

For many years, Radford was involved in banking, including a stint at the old Hibernian Savings Bank. He had previously worked at the National Bank of California. Over time, he became the city's event coordinator. To that end, he chaired the grand opening party for the Los Angeles Aqueduct in 1913. The event attracted over 40,000 spectators. In preparation for the event, a 50-page booklet was produced. As might be expected, the booklet was a PR statement extoling the virtues of the aqueduct, the virtues of William Mulholland, and the growth of business in the Valley.

THE PR BOOKLET – THE COVER

He was also the playground commissioner for Los Angeles and was in charge of the July 4th celebrations in 1917. A year later, he was dead. In 1919, Los Angeles acquired a camp in the Big Bear area. The city named it Camp Radford.

Tujunga Avenue in Studio City had an interesting name. In Tongva, the word translates as "a place of the old woman." Naturally, this leads to a question. What young woman are we talking about? On a mystical basis, are we talking about "Mother Nature?" That's one view. Another view, perhaps an urban legend, suggests that there is a large rock in Little Tujunga Canyon resembling a crying, grief-stricken woman who fled to the hills and was turned to stone. No matter... In 1840, the area was the site of Rancho Tujunga. Pedro and Francisco Lopez held the land grant that encompassed the present-day Sunland and Tujunga.

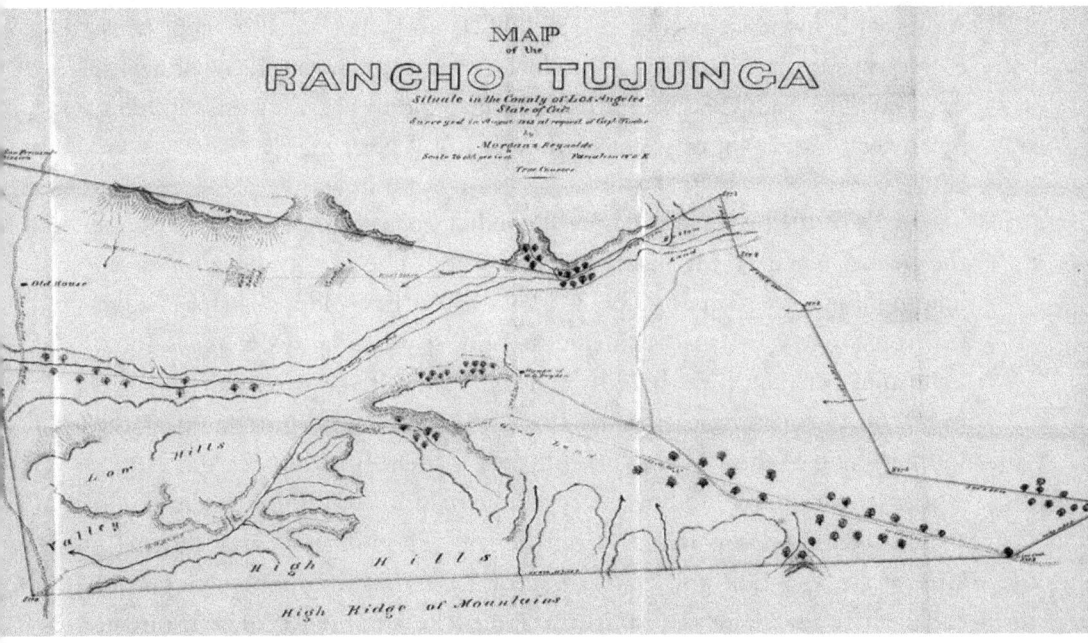

1868 MAP

CHAPTER 28 – SHERMAN OAKS

Sherman Oaks has interesting street signs with latent, if not compelling, stories. Let's take a look at some.

Benedict Canyon Drive honors Edson Abijah Benedict (1818-1886). This New York native arrived in Los Angeles in 1862 after a stop in Missouri. In downtown L.A., he went into the grocery business. Apparently, he did well enough to purchase 160 acres of Rancho Rodeo de las Aquas. The land was rugged, but that didn't stop him from building a home near Canada de los Encinos, often referred to as "Ravine of the Holy Oaks." Along with his wife Josephine (1832-1921) and their sons, he kept bees. Rumor has it that their apiary produced over 45,000 pounds of honey in one year. The bounty was sent to the Santa Monica pier for transit. That's, by any estimate, a lot of sweet stuff. Where's *Winnie the Poo*?

In 1887, the ravine was named Benedict Canyon, most likely to honor the beekeeper after his death a year earlier. The family held on to its holdings in the canyon until 1932. That's when they sold it all off. Benedict Canyon Drive was first considered in 1914. It was, if all went as planned, a shortcut between Beverly Hills and the Valley. It was eventually opened in 1926. Three years earlier, in 1923, 15.7 acres were purchased at the southern end of the canyon. The buyer was silent film star Harold Lloyd. As the first of many Hollywood types, he paid $100,000 for the land. He then built a 44-room mansion on the site. The mansion was known as Greenacres. A 9-hole golf course and a huge swimming pool were part of the deal. It pays, one would assume, to make a name for oneself on the silent screen.

THE BEEKEEPER, THE ACTOR, THE MANSION

Beverly Glen Boulevard was christened in 1918. Property owners in the area had petitioned for a name change, seeking to rename Orange Avenue and Brown Canyon Road. They got their way. As always, there's more to the story.

In 1910, Bertram Chapman Mayo (1865-1920) was hired to survey the hills around present-day Sherman Oaks. He did so under the auspices of the Southern Pacific Railroad. That company owned the right-of-way through the nearby canyon. The railroad was considering laying tracks from the Valley to Santa Monica. That never happened. Mayo has now changed roles. He was hired to subdivide the hills into residential lots. Here things get a bit murky. Real estate records indicate that Mayo owned a substantial parcel of land that he had purchased from a man named Smith. How convenient. Mayo hired 200 "Hindu" laborers to clear the land for streets and houses. It appears the workers were actually Sikhs. In any case, he had a two-tiered sales strategy. Most lots, always the desirable ones, were sold at full market price. The others, shall we say, less developed lots were sold for far less. The buyers had to subscribe to *Sunset Magazine* as part of the deal, which Mayo had published for the Southern Pacific Railroad.

Check out the ad below. Wow, those were the days.

Hesby Street was named after Bessie Hartsook Hesby (1993-1977. A native of Omaha, Nebraska, she relocated to San Francisco in 1910, only a few years after the 1906 earthquake. Rumors have it that she was crowned "Miss Liberty" in the 1915 Pan-Pacific Exposition held in the city. Actually, she merely portrayed Lady Liberty at a peace ceremony in Golden Gate Park in 1914. No matter… In 1917, she made headlines by suggesting that all red-blooded American girls should offer "patriotic kisses" to the doughboys headed off to the European battlefields. That appeal was considered scandalous by the more prudish. As to the soldiers… It is assumed they supported this patriotic effort to boost morale.

In time, Bessie moved to California with her husband, Fred Hartsook (1876-1930). He was a highly successful portrait photographer. At one time, he owned 20 photo studios along the West Coast. He was also a cattle rancher. In addition, he owned 3,000 acres in Kern County, equivalent to approximately 40 acres in the Valley. Hartsook Street was named after him.

Toward the end of his life, things got out of hand… An outbreak of "foot-and-mouth" disease ruined his Holstein breeding business. Unexpectedly, his photo studio venture went bankrupt. And finally, the exclusive Hartsook Inn in Humboldt County burned to the ground. That's a tough deal for anyone.

A point of interest… Bessie took over the Inn after her husband passed. That was until 1938, when it burned down for the second time.

BESSIE, FRED

PAN PACIFIC EXPOSITION

Willis Douglas Longyear (1863-141)... Ever hear of him? Probably not... That's okay... Most people, unless they are deeply into the Valley's banking history, would gaze over at the name. He came to Los Angeles in 1889 and hooked up with Security Savings Bank. Later, it would be called Security First National Bank. He started as a bookkeeper and later rose to become the bank's vice president. Over time, he invested in land, including the Longridge Estates, which were situated on an old cattle ranch he owned. In 1937, Alysmae Avenue was renamed Longridge Avenue.

The Longyear family lived on Wilshire Boulevard before moving to Beverly Drive, where they lived near Beverly Gardens Park, and a curious statue remains. The statue is of a hunter and hounds. It is also pockmarked with shell holes. Apparently, Longyear imported the statue from Europe to commemorate a World War I battle in France. Why he did that is not entirely known. He did not have a relative in the war.

THE BANKER, THE STATUE

Tennis and a street name… An unlikely combination… So what's the story? May Sutton Bundy (1886-1975) was a tennis champion. Thomas Bundy (1881-1945) was her husband and also an elite tennis player. They co-owned Cahuenga Park in 1922. There, Bundy, along with his business partner C.C. Albright, developed land in the Valley. Their development was called Sherman Oaks.

May Bundy was a notable star in her time. She won the singles and doubles matches at the 1904 U.S. Open and later the singles at Wimbledon in 1905. She became the first American to do so. After raising her family, she returned to the game and reached the Wimbledon quarterfinals at age 42. That's pretty good. May's daughter was Dorothy "Dodo" Bundy (1916-2014). Believe it or not, she played competitive tennis into her nineties. Now that is something.

Sutton Street was named in honor of May Sutton, her husband, or both of them.

CHAMPIONSHIP FORM

It should be noted that Thomas Bundy's brother was Charles Leroy Bundy (1875-1953). At one time, he cofounded the influential Santa Monica Land and Water Company, which was involved in the development of Brentwood. Bundy Drive was named after Charles, or perhaps the entire family. The jury is out.

DODO IN THE MIDDLE

CHAPTER 29 – LAKE VIEW TERRACE

Some names demand your attention. How about George Washington Hoyt (1819-11896) and his son Roscoe Augustus Hoyt (1847-1921)? Both men were two of the initial investors in the town of Pacoima. The elder Hoyt was a captain in the Civil War. The son was too young for that scrap. In the 1880s, the Hoyt family was in the area, quietly farming and occasionally earning extra cash through land sales. Hoyt Street was named after Hoyt's father in 1887. Roscoe and his wife, it seems, live near Pinney Street in Lake View Terrace.

Pinney Street was named for Dr. Elbert Pinney (1826-1914). He was an investor in a new town called Pacoima. Born in Connecticut and educated in Ohio, Pinney set up his first practice in Illinois. In 1856, the doctor and his wife, Harriet (1830-1920), moved to Texas, where slavery was legal on the eve of the Civil War. At that time, he owned five enslaved people, including two children. During the conflict, he served as a surgeon in the Confederate Army. After the conflict ended, Dr. Pinney and his family headed west, first to Missouri and then to California, where he grew oranges near Duarte. As did so many who are now honored by street signs in the Valley, he made money as a real estate speculator. He did well. In 1887, he built a Victorian hotel in Sierra Madre. The hotel came to be called the Pinney House. Today, it is a private residence.

Curiously, one of the enslaved people owned by Pinney was James Pinney (1858-1934). After emancipation, he remained with the family. He shared a home in Monrovia with the family until his death.

ROSCOE HOYT, DR. PINNEY

How about a geography quiz? Why is a street named Kamloops in Lake View Terrace? Or another street called Kelowna? Need a hint? How about B.C., and we're not talking about religious scripture? Got it? Of course, Canada...

Kamloops is located in British Columbia at the confluence of the North and South Thompson Rivers. The city was incorporated in 1883 with 500 stout residents. Today, there are about 100,000 Canadians in town. The first European explorers reached the area in 1811. A fort was established the next year and named Fort Cumcloups. Over time, that became Kamloops, the anglicized version of the Shuswap word "Tk'amlups." That, if the etymologists are correct, means "the meeting of the waters." Kamloops prides itself on being the "Tournament Capital of Canada." It hosts more than 100 sporting events, including hockey, curling, baseball, and basketball.

As to Kelowna... It is also located in British Columbia. The name is derived from the Okanagan word kilawna, meaning "grizzly bear". The city was officially incorporated on May 4, 1905. The population at that time was 600.

KAMLOOPS AND KELOWNA

A little historical trivia... In 1911, a distinguished visitor came to Kelowna. He was fundraising. For what, you're asking? To assist Chinese citizens in revolting against those who controlled China. His name was Dr. Sun Yat-sen. But why fundraise in Canada? At the time, 15% of the population was ethnically Chinese.

DR. SUN-YAT-SEN

On August 6, 1869, Kelowna was hit by a sonic boom. Who was the culprit? Actually, an American lying too low while doing stunts as a Blue Angel... He accidentally broke the sound barrier and over $250,000 worth of glass in town. The jet was a pain in the backside in more ways than one.

Now, how did Kamloops and Kelowna Streets in Lake View Terrace get their names? That honor goes to Peter Henry Haack (1856-1915) and his wife, Mathilda (1864-1956), who was born in Canada and wanted to retain a bit of her cultural (if not geographical) heritage. Real estate records indicate they owned a ranch in the Lake View Terrace area near where the two streets originated. Peter met Mathilda in British Columbia, where they married, produced one child, and then fled southward to California to evade unpaid debts. In downtown Los Angeles, they ran a boarding house, which provided a modest income. Then they entered the real estate business, purchasing numerous properties in LA and 6,000 acres in Tulare County, Central California. At the time of his death, Peter was worth more than a million dollars. That's a lot of moolah. One wonders if Peter ever paid off his Canadian debts?

A Personal Note

In 2003, my wife and I took a 10,562-mile round-trip to Alaska, the Yukon, and Canada. We did so in our RV, which averaged about 10-11 miles per gallon of gasoline. It was a time of adventure and discovery over three months of trekking as far north as the Arctic Circle (about five miles past the line). Due to the vast distances involved, we divided up the driving on a 3-to-1 basis. This brings us to Kamloops. We were about 50 miles from the town, and Jan was driving, as it turned out, into the worst snow blizzard we encountered on our trip. You could not see more than five feet ahead of you. The snowflakes floated down in a torrent of whiteness, obscuring all visibility. Not knowing what lurked off the road, we were fearful of getting off the road. Staying on the road meant the menace of large trucks colliding with us. Eventually, we saddled up to one of those monster vehicles, staying behind it just close enough to keep its rear lights in view. And that's how we got to Kamloops. My wife earned her stripes that day.

In 1917, Lincoln Street was renamed Osborne Street. Why was that? The answer begins with Henry Zenas Osborne Sr. (1848-1923). What was his claim to fame? He was an itinerant newsman from New York who, accompanied by his family, came to Los Angeles in 1884. In time, he commenced a 13-year career as the editor of the *Los Angeles Evening Express*. He excelled in the newspaper business and later ventured into politics, ultimately finding a home in the U.S. House of Representatives in 1916. He served until he died in 1923. So, what is Osborne Street named after? Well, not exactly.

Osborne senior has two sons, Sherrill Blasdel Osborne (1873-1949) and Henry Zenas "Harry" Osborne Jr. (1875-1948). Both were involved in real estate, subdividing land in the Pacoima area. Sherrill did well and eventually became the mayor of Eagle Rock. Harry was the chief engineer of the Los Angeles Board of Public Utilities. It appears Osborne Street was named after the brothers, with the dad lurking somewhere in the past.

THE SENIOR OSBORN

CHAPTER 30 – MOVIE MAGIC AND THE VALLEY

In 1930, a movie was filmed in the Porter Ranch area. It was called *Billy the Kid*. To do so, a Western town was built by MGM north of today's Devonshire Street. The film appears to be the first movie production in that part of the Valley. In appearance, it tried to duplicate Lincoln County, New Mexico. How about that!

Lincoln County was the home of William Bonney, better known as Billy the Kid. King Vidor directed the film. Johnny Mack Brown starred as Billy, while Wallace Beery played the role of Sheriff Pat Garrett, the lawman who put the youthful gunslinger on Boot Hill. The film was based on Noble Burroughs' 1925 book, *The Saga of Billy the Kid*. The plot was basic. Billy worked for an English rancher named Jack Tunston and was pursued by Garrett. Why was the sheriff after Billy? The young man had shot and killed a land baron who had killed Billy's boss. The sheriff chases after Billy, who is headed for Mexico. The sheriff must decide what to do with the "Kid" once he is captured—bring him in or let him go?

1930 POSTER, BERRY AND BROWN

KING VIDOR DIRECTING

LINCOLN COUNTY, NEW MEXICO IN PORTER RANCH (1930)

————————————

The *Karate Kid* (1984) was an instant hit on the wide screen as well as in our hearts. We all remember the stars, Ralph Macchio (Daniel LaRusso) as the troubled boy, and Pat Morita (Mr. Miyagi) as his mentor and friend.

Columbia Pictures decided to make the picture due to the success of *Rocky* (1976) years earlier. Same sort of plot... The underdog rises against all odds to beat the bully. The film would gross over $ 130 million. It was Hollywood's biggest sleeper film of the year.

THE TEACHER, THE STUDENT

The movie was filmed primarily in and around Los Angeles, including Reseda, Canoga Park, Woodland Hills, and Malibu. More to the point, Daniel LaRusso's apartment was located at 18223 Saticoy Street. Mr. Miyagi's house was filmed at 20924 Gault Street. Additionally, Charles Evans Hughes Jr. High School in Woodland Hills and Leo Carrillo State Beach were used for filming. Now get this... The All-Valley Karate Championship was filmed at California State University (CSUN).

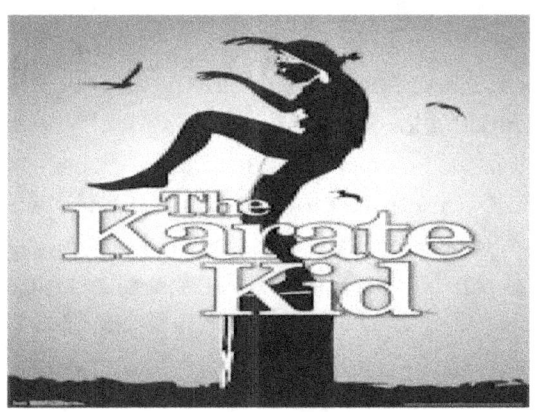

––––––––––––––

Encino Man was a 1992 American comedy film. In the movie, two lively teenagers discover and then thaw out a frozen troglodyte. They all have to adjust to each other. Sean Astin starred alongside Brendan Fraser, Mariette Hartley, and Paul Shore. The $7,000,000 budget was modest. The return was terrific. The film grossed over $40,000,000. The film is today considered a cult classic.

The filming locations included Los Angeles Mission College in Sylmar and Six Flags Magic Mountain. The family home in the film was at 7532 Sedgwick Court in West Hills. For those into details… The minimart scene was shot at 6568 Van Nuys Boulevard in Van Nuys.

SEAN ASTIN

––––––––––––––

The next movie was filmed primarily in the Los Angeles area, especially in the San Fernando Valley, including Porter Ranch, Northridge, Tujunga, and Culver City. Other locations include Redwood State Park near Crescent City in Northern California. Can you guess what films? Hint: Elliot's house was located at 7121 Lonzo Street in Tujunga. Last hint: Two letters in the film title have become part of American culture. You got it… Yes, *E.T., The Extra-Terrestrial (1982)*, Steven Spielberg's classic production and box office hit. The $10,500,000 budget brought in $790,000,000. That's a lot of bangs for a buck.

We all know the story. Elliott befriends a visitor from beyond our Solar System, an extraterrestrial whom he calls E.T. Stranded on Earth, E.T. needs a friend as he seeks a way to return home. The boy and his friends help make that happen after a series of adventures that brought tears and laughter to audiences worldwide. We still remember the stars of the film, including:

Henry Thomas as Elliott, the 10-year-old boy.
Drew Barrymore as Gertie, the younger sister.
Robert MacNaughton as Michael, the older brother.

THE KIDS

Dee Wallace as May Taylor, the single mother.
Peter Coyote as Keys, the government agent after E.T.

THE MOHER AND FRIEND, THE HUNTER

SPIELBERG AND E.T.

A Personal Note

As with many parents, I took my children to the movies. It was almost always a great experience --- soft drinks, popcorn, Milk Duds, and acceptable tears and laughter befitting the flick we were watching. This was undoubtedly true of Spielberg's E.T. film. The kids loved it. I love it. Their mother loved it. Unanimity in any family is to be treasured. We did. The kids are grown up now and off on their own. Each year, however, we pull out our old DVD and once again wait for E.T. to say, "Be good."

Fast Times at Ridgemont High is now a cult classic. Produced in 1982, this coming-of-age comedy hit a receptive nerve with young and old alike. It starred Sean Penn and Jennifer Jason Leigh, among others, as their school lives, both on and off campus, are followed. Naturally, a high school was needed for production. That school turned out to be Van Nuys High School. Many scenes were shot there as well as in the Sherman Oaks Galleria. The modest budget for the film was $4,5000,000. It earned $27,100,000. That's a pretty nice return on the investment. In 2004, the film was selected for preservation by the Library of Congress for being "culturally, historically, or aesthetically significant."

THE FILM, VAN NUYS HIGH

The film featured many songs. One that fully captured a young man's heart was *Somebody's Baby.*

Well, look at that girl with the lights coming up in her eyes
She's got to be somebody's baby
She must be somebody's baby...

All the guys on the corner stand back and let her walk on by
She's got to be somebody's baby
She must be somebody's baby
She's got to be somebody's baby, she's so fine...

She's probably somebody's only light.
Gonna shine tonight
Yeah, she's probably somebody's baby, alright...

The shooting of this film took place in Denver, Colorado, as well as in Albuquerque, Santa Fe, and Taos, New Mexico. Production was also in Bakersfield, North Hollywood, San Fernando, Sun Valley, and Van Nuys. Talk about needing a road map... The critical response to the film was overwhelmingly negative. The film was described as "sloppily made, the villains are pathetic cartoon characters.' Another critic said: "One can forgive the orangutan's participation --- he couldn't read the script --- but what's Eastwood's excuse?" Touted like that, you might think the film tanked at the box office. Actually, the film starring Clint Eastwood grossed over $ 104,000,000 and was the fourth-highest-grossing movie of 1978. In other words, Every Which Way but Loose was a resounding financial success, the critics notwithstanding.

THE STARS, THE FILM POSTER

In 1976, filming began at Mason Park in Chatsworth, California. Soon, the cameras were at work at the intersection of Sunset Boulevard and North Mapleton Drive, as well as at Flooky's Bat-A-Ball in Sherman Oaks (14661 Ventura Boulevard to be exact). That's where the team put in hitting practice. Additional work was done at the Los Angeles City Hall. Of course, the film was *The Bad News Bears*, a team that was sponsored by a fictionalized local company, "Chico's Bail Bonds."

THE BAD NEWS BEARS

LOOKY'S BAT-A-BALL

This sports comedy was a sort of *Karate Kid* story, set in the world of baseball, featuring cleats, a bat, and a glove. Upstart, apparently unqualified youths, distained by others and rejected as losers, find their way to win, notwithstanding their coach, an alcoholic ex-baseball pitcher. That is, of course, Walter Matthau. Led by Tatum O'Neal and a group of feisty players, the team overcomes great odds, now led by a manager who begins taking the kids seriously. In the end, they make it to the championship game.

TATUM AND MATTHAU

Westerns are exciting. Galloping horses, six-guns blazing away, and bad guys in black hats getting what they deserve. Roy Rogers made a number of those films, including *The San Fernando Valley* (1944), which was set in the Valley and filmed at the Iverson Ranch in Simi Valley.

Westerns often have a song. With Roy Rogers and Dale Evans at the peak of their popularity, that was undoubtedly the case. Who can forget their tribute to the San Fernando Valley?

I'm packing my grip
And I'm leaving today
'Cause I'm takin' a trip
California way
I'm going to settle down and never roam again
And make the SAN FERNANDO VALLEY my home.

I'll forget my sins
I'll be makin' new friends
Where the West begins
And the sunset ends
'Cause I've decided where yours truly should be
And it's the SAN FERNANDO VALLEY for me.

––––––––––––

Comedies make us laugh as we watch the human race go through its humorous antics. *Earth Girls Are Easy* (1988) comes to mind, another film made in the Valley. Who can forget the aliens played by Jim Carrey, Damon Wayans, and Jeff Goldblum, and their romances with Earth girls? The film locations included the Griffith Observatory, Ted and Valerie's house at 19625 Bryant Street in Northridge, and Randy's Donuts in Inglewood.

One of the film's songs was *Earth Girls Are Easy*. The lyrics explained all:

On the edge of outer space
I chanced upon a mysterious place
I dropped in, checked it out
Alien girls were all about
Eons since I had a date
Another light year's too long to wait

Earth girls
Earth girls are easy
Earth girls
Know how to please me
Earth girls

And these girls are loads of fun
Even hotter than the sun
Well, I've had lots of girls
Most of them are from other worlds
While shooting through the galaxy
The valley girls are the ones for me, yeah.

———————

Filmgoers also enjoy a dramatic moment when love and a panorama of human emotions explode on the screen, as in *Dancing at the Blue Iguana* (2000), another Valley production. This film about the lives of strippers at a strip club in Los Angeles takes place mainly in the San Fernando Valley, as well as on the seedy Sunset Strip at the Crazy Girls Strip Club. Dramatic films come in many forms.

But not to be forgotten is the horror tale…People love to be scared out of their wits. Sometimes it's the evildoer lurking in the shadows… At other times, it's the unearthly creature from another planet intent on harming earthlings. Science fiction films, what a genre… They lend themselves to scariness. Who can forget *Invasion of the Body Snatchers* (1978), when pods slowly took over human forms and consciousness? And then, of course, there were the *Alien* films with unending sequels. Everything is possible in science fiction movies. And that's the case in the next movie filmed in the Valley.

Plan Nine from Outer Space (1956) was shot originally under the shooting title, Grave Robbers from Outer Space. It premiered at the Carlton Theater in Los Angeles. A year later, it was more widely distributed. Several locations were involved around Southern California, including Palmdale, Victorville, and the Mojave Desert, all eerie and mysterious places under the right circumstances, with haunting music. The older man's house in the film was in Sylmar, at 15129 Lakeside Street. The scary cemetery scenes took place at the Pioneer Memorial Cemetery in Sylmar (14451 Bledsoe Street). The film produced by Ed Wood had an extraordinary budget of $60,000. The Baptist Church of Beverly Hills funded the project in an "ill-advised attempt to get into the film business."

THE MODEL FLYING SAUCER FOR THE FILM

Lots of movies were filmed in the Valley. With so many ideal locations, why not? Hollywood took note. At least 35 films found their way into the San Fernando Valley. Pass the popcorn.

CHAPTER 31 – COOL MUSEUMS IN THE VALLEY

Mission San Fernando Rey de España is in Mission Hills. It was founded on September 8, 1797. It was the seventeenth of the twenty-one missions established in Alta California. The mission's significance was determined by its location. It closed the gap between Mission Basilica San Buenaventura (1782) on the coast and Mission San Gabriel Arcangel (1771) in the interior. The San Fernando Mission became a popular stopping point for those traveling the El Camino Real.

THE MISSION – 1860

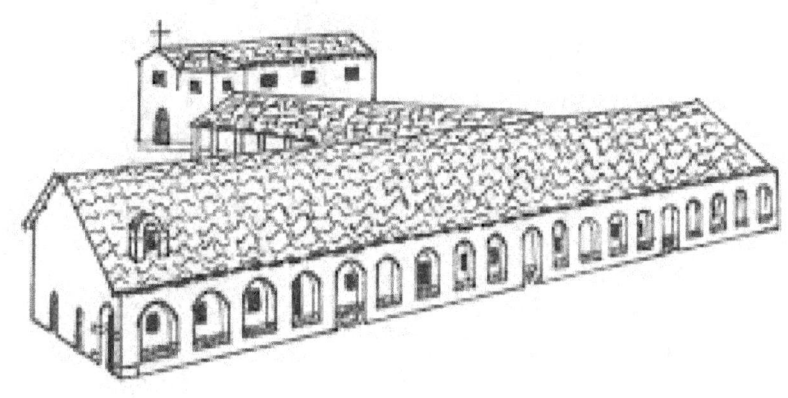

MISSION SAN FERNANDO REY

DIAGRAM OF THE MISSION

THE COLONADE

The Mission is located at 15151 San Fernando Mission Boulevard. Admission is $10.00, a reasonable sum to travel back in time, either with a guided tour or with a pamphlet in hand for a self-guided visit. The Mission is open 9:00 a.m. to 4 p.m. The Mission's phone number is 818-361-0186. There is much to see in the Mission and across the street, where a statue of Father Junípero Serra stands. Don't miss it. This Spanish Franciscan priest was the driving force behind the establishment of the California missions.

FATHER JUNIPERO SERRA, A PASTORAL LIFE LONG GONE

A personal note

Over a decade ago, my grandson came to me with a special request. He was in the fourth grade at the time, and his teacher had given him a very special assignment. He had to research and photograph something tied to California's history. With that in mind, he decided to find out about Mission San Fernando. He wanted my assistance in doing so. On one Saturday, camera in hand, we visited the mission and toured and photographed every room. In the process, he also took notes and discussed everything with me. It was a memorable day, one to make a grandfather's heart jump with joy. We capped it off with burgers at Bob's Big Boy.

What could be better? Somewhere, I hoped Father Serra was delighted in our day.

The Valley Relics Museum is located at the Van Nuys Airport in Hangars C #3 and 4 in Lake Balboa. The exact address is 7900 Balboa Boulevard, Lake Balboa, 91406. The entrance is off Stagg Street. The museum is open only on Saturdays and Sundays, from 10:00 a.m. to 3:00 p.m. There is a $15 admission fee. The museum features a vast collection of historical artifacts related to the San Fernando Valley. The exhibits feature a wide array of pop culture, including fast cars, neon signs of every description, and those of restaurants such as Mel's Drive-In, Dairy Queen, and Bob's Big Boy. If you're into high-end shopping, there are excellent examples of Tiffany signs.

THE HANGARS

A Personal Note

Growing up in San Francisco, I joined my high school buddies to go to Mel's Drive-In on Friday nights. It's what you did. It was cool being in a friend's car, finding a parking space, and ordering burgers, shakes, and fries —the gastronomic delight of adolescent cast-iron stomachs. It was also a spot to ogle, and not just at the menu.

When traveling across the country with our children, we always had a family ritual. As we drove into town, the kids were on the lookout for Dairy Queen. Once spotted, we careened off the main road to partake of milkshakes, root beer floats, and a bucketload of fries… Ah, the good old days.

Going to Bob's Big Boy was always a treat. We took numerous pictures of the kids standing proudly next to the Big Boy statue in front of the restaurant. Of course, I had *a special fondness for the place, since we shared the same first name.*

The Museum of the San Fernando Valley is a must-see. It is located in Northridge at 18904 Nordhoff Street. It is on the SE corner of Nordhoff and Wilbur. The phone number is 818-347-9655. The Museum is only open on Tuesdays from 1 to 5:00 p.m. The displays provided a voice to the Valley's past, inclusive of all groups, by preserving artifacts, documents, and records. Admission is free. Talk about a great bargain—figure on spending a couple of hours.

of the San Fernando Valley

Andres Pico Adobe is also known as Rancho Romulo. It was built in 1834. This makes it the oldest residence in the San Fernando Valley and the second oldest in Los Angeles. Francisco Avila constructed the Avila Adobe in 1818. It is located on Olvera Street, which is a part of the

Los Angeles Plaza Historic District. The Andres Pico Adobe is located at 10940 Sepulveda Boulevard in Mission Hills. The home has been a living museum managed by the San Fernando Valley Historical Society since the City of Los Angeles took over the property in 1965. The restoration of the building aimed to create a 1873-style residence. The Museum is open from 10 to 4:00 p.m. on Mondays. There is no admission charge.

THE ADOBE THROUGH THE YEARS

The Los Encinos State Historic Park is located at 16756 Moorpark Street in Encino, California. It is near the corner of Balboa and Ventura Boulevards. The Park preserves the buildings of Rancho Los Encinos, especially the adobe, which was built in 1849 by Vicente de la Ossa. The rancho features the original Ossa Adobe, which has nine rooms, as well as the two-story Garnier building, a blacksmith shop, a natural spring, and a pond. The 4.7-acre site became a part of the California State Park System in 1949. This is also a living museum that replicates the period furnishings and the daily life of early settlers in Southern California. The Park is open on Wednesdays through Sundays from 10:00 a.m. to 5:00 p.m. Admission is free.

THE OSSA ADOBE, THEN AND NOW

THE GARNIER BUILDING

The Chatsworth Historical Society was founded in 1963. It is located at 10385 Shadow Oak Drive in Chatsworth. It is located on the Homestead Acre and is designated as Los Angeles Historic-Cultural Monument No. 122. The cottage is an American Craftsman Bungalow. It is situated on a 1.3-acre site in Chatsworth Park. The property is owned by the City of Los Angeles, with the Chatsworth Historical Society acting as the conservator of the buildings and land. Tours are provided on the first Sunday of every month from 1 to 4:00 p.m. The admission is a modest $5.00. Of particular interest is the Minnie Hill Palmer House, also known as Homestead Acre. It is the only remaining homestead cottage in the Valley.

The Homestead Acre • 10385 Shadow Oak Drive • Chatsworth, CA 91311 • (818) 882-5614

THE MINNIE HILL PALMER HOME

The Santa Susana Depot Museum and Model Railroad is located near the Santa Susana Pass in Simi Valley. The exact location is 6503 Katherine Road, Simi Valley. The railroad depot once served the community of Rancho Simi as a passenger station, a telegraph office, and a freight depot. Farmers shipped their crops at the depot and picked up equipment brought in by the railroad. The depot opened in 1903 and was closed in the 1970s, destined for demolition. To prevent this, the County of Ventura purchased the depot for $1.06. The building was divided into three parts and moved by truck to a property owned by the County. There it was reassembled and designated Landmark No. 29 by the County in 1976. The museum is open on the weekends from 1 to 4:00 p.m. The phone number is 805-581-3462. There is no admission fee for kids. A donation of $2.00 is recommended for adults.

THE DEPOT

_____

The Lenis Adobe and Plummer House Museum is a historic adobe located in Calabasas, California. The house is one of the oldest surviving private residences in Los Angeles County. Miguel Leonis built the home in 1844. At that time, he was a very wealthy rancher. The Museum 's address is 23537 Calabasas Road. The phone number is 818-222-6511. The Museum opened on May 21, 1966, and is open from 10:00 a.m. to 4:00 p.m. on Saturdays. The Museum is free to guests. Donations, of course, are welcome.

The Plummer House is often referred to as the "oldest house in Hollywood." It was the home of John C. Plummer and his family. Apparently, the Plummers and the Leonis families were close. Historical records indicate that. Following a fire at the Plummer house, the City of Los Angeles relocated the remaining portions of the home to the Leonc Adobe property. Over time, the Plummer House was restored and registered as State Historical Landmark #160. The drawing below describes what can be seen to make for a great self-guided tour.

Exhibits:

1. The Plummer House
2. The Bath House
3. The Tank House
4. The Windmill and Water Pump
5. The Leonis Adobe
6. The Old Oak Tree
7. The Coops
8. The Barn
9. The Wagon Collection

THE PLUMMER HOUSE

CHAPTER 32 – MUSEUMS
IN MISSION HILLS

If you go to the intersection of Brand and Sepulveda Boulevards in Mission Hills, you'll come to City of Los Angeles Marker No. 8. It tells the story of farm equipment used in the San Fernando Valley. One special exhibit is an oil tanker used by the citrus industry. It was used to fill smudge pots with oil, and once lit, the pots helped to prevent frost. There are also different types of plows and cultivators for viewing.

FARM EQUIPMENT MUSEUM

There are nine other markers within walking distance of this first marker. So let's take a walk. In just a few steps, there is a marker for the Shanty Railroad (Marker No. 7). The Southern Pacific Railroad had a shanty, sometimes known as a watchman's or signalman's shanty. It was a little more than 5x9 feet, a wooden structure. The flagman or signalman had an essential job before the introduction of electronic crossing gates. It was his job to protect the railway and, of course, to alert approaching vehicles. He signaled with his lantern.

THE SHANTY

In 2022, the San Fernando Valley Historical Society, in collaboration with the City of Los Angeles, erected Marker No. 3 to commemorate and honor a bell. But not just any bell. So what's the story? The Spanish established 21 California missions across 700 miles of the Golden State. The road connecting these missions, each a day's journey by horseback, was called El Camino Real. That was Spanish for the Royal Road, or the King's Highway." To preserve this heritage, the California Bell Company was founded in 1906 to produce 90-pound bells and to cast the first 450. The first one was unveiled on Olvera Street on August 15, 1906, at the Plaza Church. The poles were 11 feet long and in the shape of a Shepherd's hook.

THE MISSION HILLS BELL

A bell can be found in Mission Hills at the intersection of Sepulveda Boulevard and Brand Boulevard. The exact address is 10940 Sepulveda. When you visit the site, think of a girl named Anna Pitcher. She resided in Pasadena. In 1892, she began a campaign to preserve El Camino Real. In time, other women joined in the effort by establishing the California Bell Company.

OUR SPANISH LEGACY

In the same vicinity there is another marker (No. 2), erected in 2022, that showcases the patio of Andres Pico Adobe, located behind the residence. The patio is used today for educational purposes. Schoolchildren learn how to make adobe bricks, churn butter, sew quilts, and spin yarn. These are all valuable skills when the lights go out in our digital civilization.

THE PATIO

Not far from the Patio is the Fountain (Marker No. 150). It is located at 11088 Columbus Avenue (the intersection of San Fernando Mission Boulevard and Columbus Avenue. The history of the Fountain dates back to 1812=1814 when a replica of one in Cordoba, Spain was built. It became part of the early water system of the San Fernando Mission garden. Over a hundred years later, the garden was owned by Leslie C. Brand. He donated part of his property to the city of Los Angeles for a park. The City took up the challenge of restoring the mission garden. The fountain was relocated bodily from its original location to its current site, a distance of 300 feet. This was one on July 4, 1922.

THE FOUNTAIN

The following site to visit is at 15151 San Fernando Mission Boulevard, near Columbus Avenue. The marker honors Fray Ferin Francisco de Lasuen (1736-1803). He was born in Victoria, Spain, and later joined the Franciscan Order in 1751. In 1759, he was sent to the College of San Fernando in Mexico City. In time, he went to Baja, California. He spent ten years at Mission San Diego before being selected to succeed Fr. Junipero Serra. He helped to establish nine missions. One of them, of course, was Mission San Fernando. A statue of de Lasuen is located in the side garden near the Diocese Archives.

THE MISSION BUILDER

CHAPTER 33 – LEGACY

The land is still here, the deep, fertile valleys and the immense fields of wheat and corn stretching across the Great Plains. The majestic snow-capped mountains, the result of geological forces beyond comprehension, still straddle the country, obstacles to some, but poetry to others. The great rivers flow endlessly across the terrain, beginning as streams, tiny tributaries of snow that, over time, become the sinews of the Mississippi, the Missouri, and the Colorado. They are all still with us, but now they have names, as do the towns and cities that dot the map, and every road and street, all of which are recorded on a map and in the digital world of satellites and navigation systems.

Much has been discovered and explored. Yet, the naming process continues all around us. A new housing development requires new addresses and names. A telescope in the sky observes stars, each demanding a name. History is reassessed, and street signs are altered to honor forgotten or neglected moments in our history. A new vocabulary is needed to comprehend the progress of science, which constantly alters our understanding of reality. The naming process continues, helping us all navigate the longitude and latitude of our lives.

The "names on the land" constitute our legacy. They are the heritage we bestow on each generation. They are and continue to be the history of the San Fernando Valley, street signs at every intersection and long every boulevard and avenue, along every road we take each day.

George R. Stewart understood this when he wrote.

The period of active naming spanned four centuries, during which customs and fashions underwent significant changes. The work was shared among all classes from the border ruffian to the Boston Brahman. It drew upon various languages and races.

Names on the Land
1945

POSTSCRIPT

The following assisted in writing this narrative of street names in the San Fernando Valley. George R. Stewart's book, *Names on the Land* (1945), provided the necessary inspiration to make this effort. As he wrote:

But most of them were little names, known only to those who lived nearby, of ponds and swamps and creeks and hills, of townships and villages, of streets and ranches and plantations, of coves and gulches and meadows. These little names arose by so many thousands that, at last, they were numbered by the millions.

The digital world of *Wikipedia* was most helpful. That free encyclopedia, given a few taps on the keyboard, provided an immense library of information that assisted in the research.

L.A. Street Names, also a digital source, provided background information and photos to enhance the written word. I am indebted to Mark Tapio Kines for his research over the years.

The Los Angeles County Public Works also provided technical background information on how streets are named. The Los Angeles Public Library linked the past to the present with historical data.

Robert Livingston
Northridge, California
2025

www.ingramcontent.com/pod-product-compliance
Lightning Source LLC
Chambersburg PA
CBHW071718120626
46550CB00001B/283